# FRANK HORNBY'S
# RAILWAY
# DIARY
## 1952-59

13 February 1954: 'Battle of Britain' 4-6-2 No 34087 *145 Squadron* – a 1948 product of Brighton Works – is having a rest day, parked on a siding at Battersea shed (see page 18).

# FRANK HORNBY'S
# RAILWAY
# DIARY
## 1952-59

### A personal record of
### railway journeys and observations

Silver Link Publishing Ltd

This book is dedicated to those life-long friends whose
company made many of these outings described so enjoyable:

Alan Pike OBE
The late Norman Browne
The late Peter Saxby
The late Raymond Phillips

First published in 2009

British Library Cataloguing in Publication Data

A catalogue record for this book is available from the
British Library.

ISBN 978 1 85794 332 0

Silver Link Publishing Ltd
The Trundle
Ringstead Road
Great Addington
Kettering
Northants NN14 4BW

Tel/Fax: 01536 330588
email: sales@nostalgiacollection.com
Website: www.nostalgiacollection.com

Printed and bound in the Czech Republic

The author and publisher are grateful to Zoe White for
transcribing the original manuscript diaries.

# PREFACE

My lifelong passion for railways was
stimulated at a very early age by the
Christmas gift of a clockwork train set, to
which, during the next few years, many items
were added, the majority being the products of
my namesake's Liverpool factory!
Locospotting outings with school friends
commenced in the late 1930s, initially near to
my home in the vicinity of Clapham Junction,
but taking in the London termini soon
afterwards. Then came the war and a
temporary cessation to such activities, but after
the 'blitz' subsided journeys were made further
afield, in crowded trains, aided by some pocket
money from my first weekly wages.

I then began to keep a record of my travels –
even, in an abbreviated form, while serving in
the Army in Italy, Austria and Egypt. Within
weeks of demobilisation I toured Scotland with
a friend, taking my first photographs with a
pre-war 'Box Brownie', but eventually with
rather better equipment.

Hopefully the following extracts and
photographs will give some flavour of the
many expeditions made in those halcyon days
of the 1950s, when we still counted steam
engines in their many thousands with, latterly,
a modest infiltration of diesel and electric
traction to add still further to the variety.

I would like to acknowledge the assistance
provided by copies of *The Railway Magazine*
and *The Railway Observer*, and *Irish Railways
since 1916* by Michael H. C. Baker.

# CONTENTS

Introduction: Shed visits (1955)                                          7

21-23 May 1952          Northern Ireland                                   9
13 February 1954        Nine Elms and Battersea loco depots               18
20 February 1954        Neasden and Cricklewood loco depots               20
3 April 1954            SLS 'Tilbury Centenary' tour from Fenchurch Street 21
25 April 1954           RCTS special, Victoria to Swindon and Highworth    23
15-24 May 1954          Scottish tour                                      27
3-10 July 1954          North Wales and the Isle of Man                    46
23 April 1955           Nine Elms and Battersea loco depots                57
20-22 May 1955          South Wales tour                                   61
6 August 1955           North and East London                             68
20 August 1955          London area                                       69
10-13 June 1956         North East England tour                           71
7-16 July 1956          South Devon tour                                   83
9 March 1957            Tonbridge                                          95
16 March 1957           East Grinstead                                     97
5 October 1957          Hitchin                                            98
3 May 1958              Watford and Stratford                            100
17 May 1958             A Kentish contrast: Ashford and the RH&DR        105
31 May 1958             Lincolnshire and Nottinghamshire                 109
13 September 1958       Norfolk                                          113
18 May 1959             Wellingborough and Higham Ferrers               117
29 August-
  1 September 1959      West Midlands and Wirral                         120

Index                                                                    127

*Above* 18 June 1956: When built in 1907, 'D20' 4-4-0 No 62386 was one of the North Eastern Railway's top-link engines. Seen at York, it is leading a quieter life, on a stopping train to Harrogate.

*Below* 12 July 1956: 'A stranger in paradise'! For route-learning purposes, Southern Region 4-6-2 No 34069 *Hawkinge* is working an Exeter-Plymouth train along the coast at Teignmouth (see page 83).

# INTRODUCTION: SHED VISITS (1955)

**A**lthough pursuance of the study of railways attaches a great deal more importance these days to route coverage and photography than was the case several years ago, the recording of locomotives 'en masse' at depots and works still remains high on the agenda when the year's programme is planned.

The first visit ever made was to Old Oak Common on 27 August 1938, followed by Battersea on 3 May 1939. No complete records have been retained of these or of the majority of the unofficial wartime visits, but it was strongly noticeable on last Saturday's excursion to Battersea [see page 57] that, despite the invasion of Bulleid and BR 'Pacifics' and LMR-type tank engines, a great many of the occupants were identical to those seen 16 years ago!

During 1940 the Blitzkrieg restricted such activities, but during lulls in 1941, '42 and '43 a series of very frequent visits were made to the four depots in NW London (Willesden, Neasden, Cricklewood and Old Oak), penetration through the defences being made in that order of frequency! These 'invasions' were frequently curtailed by the vigilant guardians, but nevertheless copious observations of a very high standard of interest were put on record. The only other shed visited during this period was Southall, and this era came to an end with the 'call-up' at the beginning of 1944.

Despite the obvious restrictions imposed by military service, there were compensations, not least of which was the opportunity for spells of observation in Darlington. On 5 August 1944 the shed was explored, with permission, with a haul of 65 locos. Further visits (unofficial) were made on 28 October and 11 November 1944. During leave, on 11 September 1944, Old Oak, Willesden and Neasden were toured in the morning and part of Stratford shed was penetrated during the afternoon.

The next three years, interrupted by a short spell of home leave, were spent overseas, until I was 'liberated' on 9 September 1947.

The post-war era, which has continued uninterrupted up to the present day, began with a tour of Scotland, which, though unenterprising by more recent standards, with only ten sheds and two works visited in eight days, the selection of types seen and, for the first time, in a few instances even photographed, was exceptionally good.

It is not possible to give a chronological detailed survey of all the expeditions made since. Suffice to say that, in all, 287 out of the 343 main sheds have been visited, together with a great number of sub-depots, to which must be added the majority of the sheds in Ireland. Very few of the larger depots have been omitted, the major omissions being in the Glasgow & South Western area.

Expeditions made under the auspices of the RCTS have of course been responsible for a high proportion of these visits. The first of many coach tours was a relatively modest one from Woodford, ending at Rugby and covering the Nuneaton, Banbury and Leamington area, on 19 June 1949. Since then, outstanding examples have been the 'NE Area' tour, starting at Crewe and finishing at Doncaster, on 16-20

May 1951, during which 30 sheds were visited (Darlington twice) and five works, closely rivalled by the hectic NW tour of 19-20 July 1952 based on Crewe, when 34 sheds and three works were visited, of which 25 sheds were concentrated into one marathon Sunday!

Our own tours have been no less notable, if hardly as concentrated, and have taken us to Plymouth and Padstow in the South West, Fishguard and Neyland in South Wales, Holyhead in North Wales, and Wick in the extreme north of Scotland. In one expensive but outstanding 8-hour tour by taxi in the Glasgow area, over 500 'cops' were netted, including 105 on Polmadie, believed to be a record, while the holiday weeks in June 1950 and June 1951 covered 34 and 32 sheds respectively, mostly in the NW Midlands and Wales.

The only important works that have not been visited are Cowlairs, Kilmarnock and Inverurie, with lesser ones such as Oswestry, Barry and Newton Abbot, though it must be admitted that we barely gained entrance to the erecting shops at Stafford Road. Swindon has proved worthy of frequent pilgrimages, with Crewe as 'runner up', though unlike running sheds, where some have been frequently visited and most twice or more, many of the works have so far received one visit only.

As for the type and size of shed, respectful mention must be made of the larger NE roundhouse type such as Hull Dairycoates, Neville Hill and York, where, in the case of the former two, very few engines are ever seen in the open, a feature also of Neath and to a lesser extent of some other GW and MR sheds of this type. The vast extent of the shed yards at March, Stratford and Saltley, the filthiness of Liverpool Brunswick and the venerable ramshackle air of Oxford, Chester (WR) and Bath (S&D) come to mind, while the virtual monopoly of pre-Grouping engines noted at Kings Lynn, Polmont and Bathgate six years after nationalisation and 30 years after Grouping must be worthy of comment.

Turning one's attention to the 'long' shed from the point of view of covered area, Rugby, Newton Heath, Nine Elms, Eastleigh and Gorton come to mind, where the systematic 'down every other road' never seems to come to an end.

But it is surely the smaller depot that exercises the most compelling attraction. Newport (IoW), Wadebridge and Barnstaple on the Southern, Yeovil (Pen Mill), Evesham and Whitland on the GWR, Tuxford or Oban, are places where, on a Sunday, all is peace save perhaps for one engine simmering gently.

Finally it must be remarked that save for recently at Nine Elms and Battersea, and notable exceptions at Crewe North and Derby Friargate – on my first visit – I have never missed making a 'cop' on any shed visit!

13 April 1958: This panoramic view of Brighton shed shows a variety of motive power, including the preserved LSWR 'T3' 4-4-0 No 30563 and an 'A1X' 'Terrier' in LB&SCR colours. What would 'Health & Safety' think of the spotters wandering happily across the tracks?

# WEDNESDAY 21-FRIDAY 23 MAY 1952
# NORTHERN IRELAND

*I*n the days of steam I never understood why the enthusiast periodicals
*paid so little attention to the railways of Northern Ireland, in view of*
*the great variety to be found there and their close affinity with mainland*
*railways. In particular the 'Derby' influence on the UTA locomotives in*
*its Northern Counties Committee days was common knowledge, while*
*the coaching stock of the GNR(I) was not unlike that of the former*
*GNR this side of the water. I certainly had no cause to regret the three*
*visits I made there in the 1950s, of which this was the first.*

### WEDNESDAY 21 MAY 1952

We travelled from Enniskillen to Ballyshannon in GNR(I) Railcar C2, towing a very small four-wheeled wagon without buffers. Despite the sometimes grassy track we made good speed between stations, although the acceleration of these railcars is not outstanding. At Bundoran Junction a curious track arrangement was noted, whereby trains for the branch swing off the main line to the right and curve to recross the main into the branch platform to the left. The Class 'PP' 4-4-0s of 1896-1911 appear to be widely used on these secondary routes. We saw No 43 at Bundoran Junction and No 71 at the Ballyshannon.

At Ballyshannon we made out way to the CDJR terminal, a simple one-platform affair with loop, goods sidings and shed and a small shed just sufficient to house one railcar.

The County Donegal Railways Joint Committee is owned by the UTA and GNR(I) jointly, but managed separately. From Strabane on the GN Omagh-Londonderry main line, the principal route leads westwards through Stranorlar and Donegal to Killybegs, on the north shore of Donegal Bay. From Donegal the branch to Ballyshannon strikes south-westerly, following the opposite shore of the bay. Another branch from Stranorlar, headquarters of the line, serves Glenties, but prohibitive costs of track repairs have made it necessary to close this branch for passenger traffic. From Strabane there are two other branches, one north-westerly to Letterkenny, terminal of the L&LSR, and another follows the eastern bank of the River Foyle to Londonderry. The distance from Strabane to Killybegs is 50¼ miles, the Killybegs branch is 19 miles long and the Ballyshannon branch is 15¼ miles, beyond Donegal in each case. The gauge is 3ft 0in.

The first section of the line was opened in 1893, others following in 1894, 1900 and 1905. The Strabane-Derry line is, in theory, a separate company, and was opened in 1909. The Stranorlar-Donegal line had been opened throughout 1889 under the title 'West Donegal Railway'.

The present steam motive power consists of two types of 2-6-4T, five of Class 5 being built in 1907, three of Class 5a in 1912, and a third class of 4-6-4Ts, four engines of Class 4 being built in 1904, all by Nasmyth, Wilson & Co. The only engine not now running is No 7 of Class 5, withdrawn in 1940. The locomotives are painted Geranium red, and the passenger carriages, of which there are nearly 40 bogie coaches, are red with white upper panels.

In 1926 the first petrol railcars were introduced, followed by diesels in 1931, since when a fleet of these vehicles has gradually replaced most steam passenger workings, excepting on the Strabane-Derry line.

We travelled from Ballyshannon to Donegal in car 15, built by Walker Bros in 1936, bodywork from Dundalk Works. At Donegal, where there are two platforms connected by an overbridge, and some sidings, we changed into a modern car,

No 20, for the run to Killybegs. A shed, which probably once housed locomotives, at Donegal is now a bus garage. The Ballyshannon branch is undulating, with a ruling gradient of 1 in 60, but no very high summits. The Killybegs branch has a succession of switchbacks with a ruling gradient of 1 in 40, but once again the longest gradient is less than 2 miles. At Inver car 16 of 1936 was passed, and at Donegal, on the return trip, No 12, built at Dundalk in 1934 with a Gardner 74hp engine.

Numerous interesting and antique signals were seen, including 'fixed distants' consisting of a yellow arm nailed to a post, and other signals of the diamond type, which can be rotated, were noted. The halts are simple in the extreme, but the more important stations are clean, substantial and adequate. At Killybegs the platform, and the parallel loop line, are protected by a wooden roof, while there are several sidings and a turntable, constructed from the frames of a 2-6-4T. The railcars are single-ended, and all those we saw in service have an articulated front end mounted on a four-coupled power bogie.

At Killybegs 4-6-4T No 11 *Erne* arrived with a mixed train, but we did not see any other steam engines at work on the main line.

21 May 1952: County Donegal Railways bogie passenger stock at Strabane station, with railcar No 18 on the left.

Between Donegal & Stranorlar we climbed through the wild and picturesque Barnesmore Gap, a 10-mile climb at mostly 1 in 60 with some shorter lengths varying from 1 in 50 to level, followed by 1½ miles level and a 5-mile drop at 1 in 50 to 1 in 60.

Stranorlar has a sizeable station, with two platforms and a bay, goods and carriage sheds and sidings, a locomotive depot and repair shops. During a brief halt we noticed 2-6-4T No 5 shunting, Nos 1/3/8 and 4-6-4T No 9 in the shed, while the work was shared by 2-6-4T No 4 and railcar 14 of 1935. Onwards to Strabane, the line is level and less interesting. We passed car 16 (with trailer No 6) at Castlefinn, and arrived at Strabane in pouring rain.

There are fairly large yards at Strabane, and a small loco depot where we saw 2-6-4T No 6 and railcars 18/19, as well as four-wheeled diesel tractor No 11 *Phoenix*, converted at Dundalk Works from an Atkinson Walker steam tractor built for the Clogher Valley Railway in 1928. 2-6-4T No 2 *Blanche* arrived from Londonderry.

We were hauled from Strabane to Derry in a through express from Belfast by 'S2' Class 4-4-0 No 190 *Lugnaquilla*. The GN terminus at Derry consists of two platforms, with a goods yard and loco depot outside the station, alongside the River Foyle.

## THURSDAY 22 MAY 1952

The Londonderry & Lough Swilly Railway is now entirely closed to passenger traffic, and complete closure is threatened for the forthcoming summer, so we were not able to travel on any routes. We did, however, visit the locomotive depot at Pennyburn, just beyond the Graving Dock station, and saw most of the locomotive and carriage stock. The present management is convinced that road transport can better serve the sparsely populated area, and the repair shops at Pennyburn are entirely given over to road vehicle maintenance.

From Londonderry, the line runs to Tooban Junction, about 6 miles, and the main line then swings south-west to Letterkenny, 24½ miles. The Letterkenny & Burtonpoint Extension continued for another 50 miles through Kilmacreenan and Gweedore. The whole of this line has been officially closed to passenger traffic since June 1940, but a mixed train was in fact run until recently. From Tooban Junction a branch runs northward to Buncrana, and continued to Cardonagh, 30¼ miles, until 1935, when the Buncrana-Cardonagh section was closed. Passenger services ran on the Derry-Buncrana section until 6 September 1948.

The locomotive stock consists of two 4-8-4Ts, Nos 5/6, built by Hudswell Clarke in 1912, three 4-6-2Ts, Nos 8/15/16, built in 1899-1901 (No 7 was withdrawn in 1940), 4-6-2T No 10

built in 1904 (No 9 was withdrawn in 1940), three 4-6-0Ts, built for the L&BER in 1902, Nos 2-4 (No 1 was withdrawn in 1928), and 4-8-0 tender engine No 12 of 1905, No 11 having been scrapped in 1933. The 4-8-0 and 4-8-4Ts are unique in the British Isles.

We saw both the 4-8-4Ts, all three surviving 4-6-2Ts, Nos 8/15/16, and two of the three 4-6-0Ts, Nos 2/4. The 4-8-0 No 12 was unfortunately at Letterkenny, as was presumably 4-6-0T No 3 and 4-6-2T No 10. The two-road shed held most of the engines, in excellent condition, but 4-6-2T No 16 was partially dismantled. No 8 was working the morning freight train to Buncrana.

By contrast, the three-track GNR shed seemed tame, despite the foreman's willing cooperation in shunting the occupants into photographable positions. 'P' Class No 26, 'PP' No 43, 'PG' No 103, 'SG3' No 96, 'S2' Nos 190/92 and 'SG2' No 183 were on shed.

We travelled the full length of the UTA main line from Derry to Belfast (York Rd), on the 1.10pm as far as Ballymena, where we broke our journey to visit the shed, continuing on the 3.50pm thence to Belfast. From Londonderry to Coleraine 4-4-0 No 79 of Class 'U2', *Kenbaan Castle*, was the engine, and 'W' Class 2-6-0 No 102 took over, having taken the 11.05am from Derry.

Apart from the main line just mentioned, the UTA at present consists of the branch from

22 May 1952: Londonderry & Lough Swilly Railway 4-6-0T No 2 (Andrew Barclay, 1902) at Londonderry Pennyburn depot, a year before closure.

Coleraine to Portrush, the line to Larne, which branches off from the Derry route at Greenisland, and the ex-BCDR line from Queens Quay station, Belfast, to Bangor; parts of the Derry Central line from Cookstown Junction to Cookstown, and Magherafelt to Macfin (on the Belfast side of Coleraine) are still open to goods traffic.

The NCC section of the UTA was originally owned by the MR of Great Britain, and passed into LMS ownership in 1923. In most respects, particularly those of locomotives and rolling stock, the 'Derby' influence is very strong. The present motive power roster consists of 15 Class 'W' 2-6-0s introduced in 1933, the 'WT' Class 2-6-4 tank counterpart, at present 28 strong, 18 Class 'U2' 4-4-0s, a few 'A1' Class 4-4-0s, three 0-6-0s, two 0-6-0Ts, which were transferred from the LMS in 1944, and a few diesels. The principal shed and works are at York Rd, Belfast, with other depots at Ballymena, Coleraine, Larne and Londonderry.

In addition to the routes mentioned, the 3-foot-gauge lines from Ballymoney to Ballycastle, and Ballymena to Larne, are still in existence, and it is believed that occasional freight trains are run, but the four remaining 2-4-2 compound tanks are reported to be stored at Ballycastle.

Although there are only two platforms, the Londonderry UTA terminus is quite imposing, with a small two-track shed alongside. This contained 'WT' No 55 and 'U2' Nos 75/79. Another 'WT', No 4, was shunting. No 79 backed onto our train – about five vehicles – and we made a smart run to Coleraine, although we called at all stations from Limavady Junction.

There are six 'down' and five 'up' through trains in the current weekday timetable, and various additional trains over sections of the journey. One train down from Derry conveys through coaches to Larne via Greenisland, where, before the opening of the 'Loop' in the early '30s, all trains between Belfast and Derry had to reverse. Although average speeds are not unduly high, we experienced some very brisk running, with sustained 60mph bursts between Coleraine and Ballymena, behind 'W' No 102. A few miles after leaving Derry the route is

single-track to Coleraine, but, as on some GNR lines, one track of every loop is straight, and signalled for 'both way' running. Signalling is generally identical with that in England, including colour-light installations out of Belfast and at Coleraine, but level crossing warning signals with a disc at the end of the arm are a novel feature.

The 2-6-0s and 2-6-4Ts are standard in many respects with the Fowler 4P 2-6-4Ts of the LMS, and the 'U2s' are almost identical with the 2P 4-4-0s.

The shed at Coleraine contained only one engine, but Class 'A1' 4-4-0 No 66 *Ben Madigan* and 'U2' Class Nos 78/84 were noted. At Ballymoney we saw an assortment of rolling stock in the narrow gauge sidings.

We visited the shed at Ballymena, a two-road depot where about seven engines are stationed. 'W' No 98 was out of service with a cracked frame, and other locos of particular interest were two BCDR 4-4-2Ts Nos 213/30, in green livery and withdrawn from service. Two 'A1' 4-4-0s, Nos 62 *Slemish* and 69 *Slieve Bane*, were also in store.

We continued to Belfast in railcar No 4, with raised driving cabs at either end. Like the GNR railcar, acceleration was poor, but a good maximum speed was attained. Even on the UTA, perhaps the best equipped of all the Irish Railways, some sections of track were green with weeds. Several stretches of concrete sleepers were noted.

On arrival at York Rd station, Belfast, which, although quite small, seemed to be busier than any we saw in Ireland, we visited the locomotive shed and works. The latter, just beyond the end of the platforms, at right-angles to the running lines, is very small, and the four engines under repair occupied all the available space.

The running shed is a four-track double-ended type with mechanical coaler. Apart from a good selection of 4-4-0s, 2-6-4Ts and 2-6-0s, all three 0-6-0s and the diesels were seen, and ex-LMS 'Jinty', Class 'Y', No 19. Two BCDR tanks, Nos 216/17, the former partially dismantled, were seen. Class 'A1' 4-4-0 No 58 was out of service at the end of the yard.

*Above* 22 May 1952: Nearest in this line of 'dumped' engines at Ballymena shed is UTA (ex-NCC) 'A1' 4-4-0 No 69 *Slieve Bane*, with ex-Belfast & County Down 4-4-2Ts Nos 213 and 230 at the rear.

*Below* 22 May 1952: UTA diesel railcar No 4 of 1938 vintage at Ballymena. Note the driver's 'turrets' at either end.

*Above* 22 May 1952: At Belfast (York Road) UTA shed, Class 'V' 0-6-0 No 13 of 1923 is in the foreground, with 'County Down' 4-4-2T No 217 at rear.

*Below* 22 May 1952: On loan to the UTA from its builder, Harland & Wolff, is 500hp diesel No 28 shunting at Belfast (York Road). It was built for the BCDR in 1937 and scrapped in 1973.

*Above* 22 May 1952: Ten 2-6-4Ts of Class 'WT' were built at Derby in 1946-47 for the UTA Belfast-Larne services. This is No 5 at York Road shed.

*Below* 22 May 1952: UTA No 18 is one of the two LMS 3F 0-6-0Ts transferred to the NCC and regauged in 1944. It was originally LMS No 7456 and is also seen at Belfast (York Road).

In the evening we travelled from Belfast (Queens Quay) to Bangor and back on the only route of the BCDR remaining open, after visiting the locomotive depot.

The BCDR also operated routes to Newcastle, with branches from Ballynahinch Junction to Ballynahinch, from Downpatrick to Ardglass and from Newcastle to Castlewellan, there making an end-on junction with the GNR by which the latter gained access to Newcastle. Another branch ran from Comber to Donaghadee. Since the war all these routes have been replaced by bus services. Most of the locomotive stock is still intact although, as previously related, several of the 4-4-2Ts are in store. The 2-4-2Ts have been scrapped, and only two of the 0-6-0s were seen. All three of the large 4-4-2Ts of the '8' Class were seen on shed (No 9, built in 1945, was possibly the last engine of this type to be built anywhere in the world). 0-6-0 No 214 was shunting, and No 210 shared a small brick shed with 2-4-0 No 206.

The running shed has four tracks, and contained, apart from three of the 4-6-4Ts, many of the 4-4-2Ts and the 0-6-4T No 229, a GN 'T1', No 187, and UTA 'WT' Nos 10/50. The repair shops have been closed. The doom of most of the engines has been sealed, however, by the appearance of three-car diesel railcar sets with Leyland engines. We travelled in one of these to Bangor, and it made light work of the switchback grades of the double-track line. By contrast the return journey was made in an elderly eight-wheeler, part of a train of four or five such vehicles hauled by 4-4-2T No 211. This veteran made some very agile descents of the banks, and we enjoyed an exhilarating run.

Bangor station has a modern exterior and three platforms, and there is a small locomotive shed. The greater proportion of BCDR stock has been repainted in UTA green, and the six-wheelers were seen in store at various stations on both the BCDR and the NCC lines.

## FRIDAY 23 MAY 1952

Great Victoria Street Station, Belfast, is quite extensive, with separate sections for arrivals and departures. We travelled out to Adelaide in a local train hauled by 'S2' 4-4-0 No 191, running tender-first. Numerous of the 'T2' Class 4-4-2Ts are stationed at Adelaide shed for this type of traffic.

The depot has about 12 tracks but, being a weekday, only 30 engines were seen, of which the most interesting was Dundalk, Newry & Greenore Railway 0-6-0ST No 1 *Macrory*, the only survivor of the LNWR tanks that worked this line. The four others were at that time awaiting scrapping at Sutton, near Howth. Three of the four 0-6-4Ts of Class 'RT' were also seen. These work on the dock lines, and are built to a restricted loading gauge. UTA No 57 of Class 'WT', on loan to the GNR, was noted.

We travelled out to Lisburn in diesel railcars 614/15, and thence to Portadown in 606/07. At Portadown, a junction with four platforms, the shed is a 12-stall ferro-concrete roundhouse identical with that at Clones, and with an allocation of about 15 engines, mainly 0-6-0s and 4-4-0s of moderate size, including some of the modern 'UG' Class. There is a busy goods yard, about the size of that at Wimbledon.

No 115 of Class 'T2' hauled us back to Belfast, in a three-coach semi-fast train, which ran with typical 'GN' smartness on the non-stop Lisburn-Belfast section. These engines are tank versions of the 'U' Class 4-4-0s, introduced by Mr G. T. Glover in 1915, one of many instances of the standardisation policy adopted by the GNR.

This was our last experience of the GNR, and all that remained of our tour of Ireland was the 24.3-mile run from York Rd station to Larne Harbour for the 6.50pm boat to Stranraer. A 2-6-4T hauled us to Larne Town on the 4.55pm fast train, stopping at Mount, Carrickfergus, Whitehead and Magheramorne, and we caught a glimpse of BCDR 4-4-2T No 221 in a shed at Carrickfergus together with another unidentified loco. Numerous BCDR coaches were stored in nearby sidings. At Larne Town, which has one through platform and a bay platform, we broke our journey to visit the shed, but the latter was empty, save for 'U2' No 87 in the yard. Railcars 1 and 2, coupled together, were passed at Whitehead, where the

double-track ends. Another 2-6-4T, No 56, hauled us round to Harbour station, where we embarked on SS *Princess Margaret* (built by William Denny, Dumbarton, in 1931) for the 2-hour, 37-mile run to Stranraer, in calm and sunny conditions.

We caught a glimpse of the Ballymena & Larne narrow-gauge depot just beyond Larne

23 May 1952: Belfast Adelaide shed was by far the biggest on the GNR(I). About to back down to Great Victoria Street terminus, is 'QS' 4-4-0 No 122.

Town, where the 3-foot-gauge track follows the broad gauge to the harbour, but apart from a few wagons nothing of interest could be seen.

So ended the great Irish tour of May 1952.

# NINE ELMS AND BATTERSEA LOCO DEPOTS

Despite the relentless progress of the withdrawal programme there is still plenty to interest the visitor at these two great neighbouring depots.

At Battersea some 60 engines were seen. The only BR Standard engine was No 70004 *William Shakespeare* in spotless condition, but there were several representatives of both 2-6-4Ts and 2-6-2Ts of LMR design. There were quite a few 'West Country' 'Pacifics', several 'Arthurs' and a couple of 'Schools' on shed. Other types were as follows: 4-4-0 Class 'E1', 0-6-0 Class 'C', 2-6-0 Classes 'N', 'U' and 'U1', 2-6-4T Class 'W', 0-6-2T Class 'E4', 0-6-0T Classes 'E2' and 'P', 0-4-4T Class 'H'. The Nestles milk siding is now shunted by a 'P' Class 0-6-0T. Longhedge Works contained three engines under repair: a 4-4-0, an 'E2' and an 'H'.

At Nine Elms, 'Pacifics' of both classes and 4-6-0s of 'Lord Nelson', 'King Arthur', 'S15' and 'H15' Classes were predominant, with a few 'Moguls' and a 'Schools'. Nevertheless, LSW Classes 'T9', 'D15' (No 30464), 'M7', '700' and 'O2' (No 30224), LBSC Class 'E4' and SECR Class 'D' were all represented. None of the diesel shunters or main-line engines were on shed.

13 February 1954: Diminutive ex-SECR 'P' 0-6-0T No 31555 shunts the Nestles milk siding, adjacent to Battersea shed.

*Above* 13 February 1954: Class 'N15' 4-6-0 No 30764 *Sir Gawain* was one of 16 'King Arthurs' stationed at Battersea shed at the time of this visit.

*Right* 13 February 1954: Three-cylinder 'U1' 2-6-0 No 31902 presents a bold front at Battersea shed.

# SATURDAY 20 FEBRUARY 1954
# NEASDEN AND CRICKLEWOOD LOCO DEPOTS

*This Saturday outing entailed a cycle ride from South West to North West London – one I would not contemplate today. We had no permit for either shed, but Neasden was easily accessible via the railwaymen's allotments, giving an uninterrupted view of the yard. However, a degree of caution was necessary at Cricklewood, entered through a gateway in the Edgware Road, but we explored the two roundhouses and shed yard without any encounter with authority!*

During a brief spell by the lineside at Neasden the most interesting sight was that of GW 'Hall' No 7913 going down the main line with a 13-coach empty stock train. All the local passenger trains seen were 'L1'-worked, but 'A5' No 69829 came on shed. As can be expected, the occupants of the shed were principally classes 'B1' and 'L1', with a couple

20 February 1954: No 47991 at rest at Cricklewood shed, one of the 33 'Garratts' built for the LMS by Beyer Peacock in 1927-30 for the Toton to Brent coal trains.

of 'A5s', 'N5s' and 'J11s', an 'A3', an 'M of S' 2-8-0 and two or three Ivatt 4F 2-6-0s. One of the 'B1s' was No 61206 of King's Cross (34A).

At Cricklewood a look round the shed yielded nothing at all outstanding. The following classes were represented: 2-8-0 Class 8F, 4-6-0 Class 5MT, 0-6-0 Classes 4F, 3F and 2F, 2-6-0 Class 4F, 2-6-4T Class 4MT of Fowler and Fairburn design, 2-6-2T Class 3MT of Fowler and Stanier design, 0-6-0T Classes 3F and 1F, a 'Garratt' and a 'Horwich' 2-6-0. One 0-6-0 diesel came on shed; the others were all working in the yards.

# SATURDAY 3 APRIL 1954
# SLS 'TILBURY CENTENARY' TOUR FROM FENCHURCH STREET

*A much appreciated feature introduced in the early 1950s was the railtour organised by the railway enthusiast societies, covering rare tracks and, if possible, behind unusual locomotives. This one celebrated the centenary of the London, Tilbury & Southend Railway and was my only run behind an LT&S 0-6-2T, a type normally confined to freight duties.*

The special train consisted of eight ER centre-gangway coaches and a cafeteria car, hauled throughout by LT&SR 0-6-2T No 41983 (33A).

The route taken was of considerable interest, and our first stretch of track not open to passenger traffic was entered soon after leaving Fenchurch Street, when we took the Gas Factory Junction-Bow Junction spur onto the Eastern Region (GE) main line.

Passing Stepney East we noticed that the spur to Limehouse, giving direct access from Fenchurch Street to the West India Docks line, is being removed, though of course the other side of the triangle, the 'Limehouse Curve', remains and carries a heavy freight traffic.

At Forest Gate we swung off through Woodgrange Park, to rejoin the LTSR at Barking, and then followed the old main line to

3 April 1954: Ex-LTSR 3F 0-6-2Ts were normally confined to freight duties, so were rarely seen at Fenchurch Street. No 41983 is pictured there heading the 'Tilbury Centenary' railtour special.

Tilbury. On this stretch, with numerous very large factories between us and the river, including the immense Ford works and various cement works, we glimpsed quite a few 'private owner' locomotives.

Instead of running into Tilbury (Riverside) we cut across the base of the triangle from Tilbury (W) to Tilbury (E) Junction, past the loco shed, and continued on to Thames Haven Junction, just short of Stanford-le-Hope. The Thames Haven branch, single track and 4 miles long, was opened in June 1885, and passenger traffic ceased over 40 years ago. There was one intermediate station, Mucking, of which little remains, and the terminus consisted of an island platform with station buildings hard on the waterfront. The wooden building is now derelict and completely disused, but the area is covered by an immense oil refinery, which yields a good deal of traffic to the railway. An 0-6-2T was shunting, and we have seen freight trains on numerous occasions passing Tilbury, usually headed by 4F 0-6-0s, from the branch. Numerous oil tankers were moored alongside the jetties or in the tideway. At Tilbury we had a good view of the new 29,000-ton Royal Mail liner *Orsova* with its curious funnel and single 'streamlined' mast.

Returning from Thames Haven past Tilbury once again we made our way to Romford and the ER main line, via Upminster, on the route served by the two-coach auto-trains handled by

3 April 1954: The peace of Thames Haven, which last saw a passenger train in 1909, is disturbed by the 'Tilbury Centenary' special, hauled by No 41983.

MR 0-4-4Ts from Upminster shed. Then followed a smart run along the main line to Stratford, where we took the Channelsea curve through Lea Junction and Victoria Park to Dalston Junction, where we reversed. At Victoria Park our engine had experienced difficulty in surmounting the stiff climb from Stratford, and came to a stop, fouling the junction and delaying freight trains approaching from the Bow and Hackney directions. We eventually restarted and completed the journey to Dalston Junction.

After reversal we made our way back – by now in the gathering darkness – through Victoria Park, turning south-east this time through Bow to Bow Junction (LMR), where we curved underneath the LTS main line, which we rejoined at Gas Factory Junction, arriving at Fenchurch Street about 8pm – half an hour late.

The principal alteration in the motive power situation on the LTS section has been the arrival of a batch of ten 'Standard' 2-6-4Ts, which work passenger turns with the Stanier and Fairburn engines. A few Eastern Region engines – ex-GE 0-6-0s of Classes 'J15' and 'J17' – can be seen of freight turns, and a couple are stationed at Plaistow for the purpose, but the old Johnson 2Fs are still well in evidence, with Fowler 4Fs. No fewer than 23 of the 3P 4-4-2Ts were withdrawn in 1951-2, but quite a few still remain, mostly on local work from Tilbury, while the 14 0-6-2Ts are still intact.

Incidentally, our empty stock was worked in and out of Fenchurch Street by an 'N7' in immaculate condition.

## SUNDAY 25 APRIL 1954

# RCTS SPECIAL, VICTORIA TO SWINDON AND HIGHWORTH

*Only three weeks after the 'Tilbury' tour, I was off to Swindon, courtesy of the RCTS, with the novelty of starting from Victoria behind a pair of ex-GWR 'Dukedog' 4-4-0s. Then followed a tour of the Works, a trip down a closed branch line, and the return journey behind a splendid '4700' 2-8-0. Truly a day to remember!*

A comfortable train had been provided by the Southern Region consisting of seven 'Continental' 2nd and 3rd Class coaches and a cafeteria car, which arrived at Victoria behind a smartly turned-out 'C' Class goods. The WR motive power, '90XX' 4-4-0s Nos 9011 and 9023, were doubtless making the first appearance of this class at any SR London terminus (and probably the last!).

Our route took us past Battersea sheds, underneath the Western Section main line and on to the West London extension, which we left at North Pole Junction, after a wait to let a couple of down expresses pass. Our progress down the WR main line, marred in any case by severe permanent way checks at Shrivenham, was leisurely and we were a few minutes late on a schedule allowing 154 minutes for the 80 miles from Kensington (Olympia).

At Victoria, before we started, a 'West Country' 4-6-2 was seen leaving on a Newhaven boat express, while on the Eastern Section side the up 'Night Ferry' express arrived behind No 34091 piloting 'Schools' No 30923, an unusual combination. The usual selection of 'West Country' 4-6-2s, 'King Arthurs' and 'C' Class 0-6-0s were outside Battersea sheds, and passing Lillie Bridge LTE depot battery loco Nos 31/46/58 were seen.

At Swindon, after a stop to allow the first Highworth branch party to detrain, we pulled down the main line, backed across it and ran forward to a siding alongside 'A' shops.

The usual impressive variety of locomotives

25 April 1954: This was without a doubt the only occasion when Victoria has been visited by ex-GWR 'Dukedog' 4-4-0s! Nos 9023 and 9011 are there on the 'South Eastern' side, prior to departure on the RCTS special to Swindon.

*Above* 25 April 1954: The two venerable-looking 'Dukedogs' stand at the head of the RCTS special of ex-SR stock at Swindon Works.

*Below* 25 April 1954: Past and pre-nationalisation 2-6-2Ts stand in Swindon Works yard. Nearest is BR 'Standard' Class 3 No 82005, with a GWR '5100' at rear.

was to be seen in the shops and yards. Two classes were being built, Class 4 4-6-0s and Class '3' 2-6-0s (series 75XXX and 77XXX respectively) and in addition WR '84XX' 0-6-0PTs are arriving from Bagnalls. No 75025 stood in the yard, Nos 75026/27/28 were in an advanced stage of production in 'A' shops with the frames and motion set up for 75029, alongside which stood the frames of 2-6-0 Nos 77010/11. Of this latter class, No 77009 was in the yard, 77005/07 were on shed, and we had passed No 77008 at Shrivenham on a PW train. New 0-6-0PT No 8444 had just been delivered from Bagnalls in the Works yard, with No 8441 on shed.

A third 'Standard' class was in evidence in the works, where Class 3 2-6-2T Nos 82001/02 occupied 'A' shop, with No 82005 in the yard. All these engines, originally allocated to Tyseley, have been recently transferred to Barry to work the 'interval' services on the Valley routes, and are presumably now undergoing some modification.

As the other side of the story, a dwindling stream of veterans of the unstandard or older standard classes continue to arrive for scrapping. The only occupant of 'C' shop was the last MSWJ 2-4-0, No 1336, while only one engine, 0-6-0PT No 2066, was awaiting the 'torch' at the end of the yard. A solitary 'Dean Goods', No 2411 (82B), minus tender, stood alongside 'A' shops, with the usual collection of engines awaiting decision or repairs, contrasting with the glistening machines ex-shops, among which was No 6000 *King George V*. The 'Manor' Class was represented by No 7818, and the '90XX' 4-4-0s by No 9008, while the only 'Star' Class to be seen was No 4062, inside 'A' shops. The usual collection of Welsh tank engines comprised TVR 'A' Class Nos 335/37, B&M Nos 434/35, and CR 0-6-0T No 682, with a sprinkling of 2-8-0Ts and 2-8-2Ts.

Undoubtedly the most interesting engines going through shops were Vale of Rheidol 1ft 11in 2-6-2Ts Nos 8 and 9, the latter being one of the two engines built for the Cambrian Railways in 1902 by Messrs Davies & Metcalfe Ltd, the former being a Swindon product of 1923.

25 April 1954: When 4-6-0 No 6000 *King George V* emerged new from Swindon Works in 1927 it was the 'Pride of the GWR'. Many years later, after a refit and sporting the bell acquired in the USA, it still looks deserving of that title.

25 April 1954: The Highworth branch had been closed for a year when visited by this RCTS special train. 0-6-0PT No 1366, normally used for dock shunting, provided the motive power.

Other interesting engines were Nos 2200 (89C), 2210 (89A), 4570 (83E), 4598 (83F) and 4683 (84J). Nos 4591 and 3186 were stripped to the frames and possibly have been withdrawn, as it is sometimes customary to dismantle tank engines of standard classes in the shops instead of breaking them up in 'C' shop.

The shed offered few interesting engines, only Nos 9676 (88C), 9766 (87B), 7788 (81D), 6652 (86J), 7341 (82B) and 7000 (83A) being noteworthy.

We entrained for Highworth in the Rodwell Lane siding alongside the Works, our train consisting of three non-corridor coaches hauled by 0-6-0PT No 1366, the prototype of the class introduced in 1934 for dock shunting.

Leaving the main line at Highworth Junction, 1 mile east of Swindon, the branch, which was closed to passengers in March 1953, climbs for 5½ miles, a fine view being obtained from the terminus. There were four intermediate stations or halts, all with one platform only, and Highworth itself also has a single platform with loop, and one siding serving a small goods shed. The steepest gradient, outside Highworth, is 1 in 44, and trains are subject to an overall speed limit of 25mph.

Our journey home took us along the main line to Reading behind 2-8-0 No 4707, which showed a fine turn of speed, and after a halt in the up through road we crossed onto the SR via the wartime spur and changed engines, LSWR 'H16' Class 4-6-2T No 30517 taking over. After following the normal main line through Wokingham and Ascot, with some lively running en route, we took the Virginia Water West Curve – not normally used by passenger trains – joining the Virginia Water-Weybridge line, and then the Western Section main line, which we followed to Wimbledon where we used the East Putney loop to Clapham Junction.

Here another splendidly turned-out 'C' Class – No 31480 – took over for the last lap to Victoria via Ludgate and Longhedge Junctions. During our wait at Clapham Junction 'Schools' No 30919 went through on the down Central Section main line with an empty train consisting of 12 coaches and a bogie luggage van.

Our arrival at Victoria was to time at 8.18, a fitting end to an excellent tour.

# SATURDAY 15-MONDAY 24 MAY 1954
# SCOTTISH TOUR

*A*lthough not my first visit to Scotland, the thought of 'crossing the border' always fired my imagination, especially in the days before overseas travel became popular, with the certainty of seeing many locomotive classes that never ventured further south. This tour was a real 'blockbuster', covering more than 2,000 miles of rail travel and with more than 500 steam locomotives 'copped'. Moreover, at a time when roll film was still quite expensive, I brought back a good selection of photographs, a further cause for satisfaction.

This year's tour was even more ambitious than its forerunners, as over 2,000 rail miles were covered and the most northerly rail termini in Britain, at Wick and Thurso, were visited. North of Newcastle, with the exception of the Inverness-Georgemas Junction section, hardly any ground was covered twice, and over 700 miles of new route were traversed including the spectacular West Highland, Kyle of Lochalsh and Oban lines.

Some 25 sheds were visited, all north of the border, and over 500 locomotives were booked, of which a high proportion were of pre-Grouping types.

## SATURDAY 15 MAY 1954

Little need be said of the journey to Newcastle, which actually commenced at 11.45pm on the night of Friday 14th on the down 'Tynesider', our arrival at Newcastle being about 10 minutes late at 6.27am. We travelled in a comfortable two-berth post-war 3rd Class sleeping car, and saw very little until the approaches to Newcastle were reached. After a short time our carriages were propelled into a bay platform, and during the following half-hour a good deal of early morning freight and passenger movements were observed, handled by a great variety of motive power. Numerous 'V1' and 'V3' 2-6-2Ts and one or two 'G5' 0-4-4Ts were seen on local passenger turns, with 'B1s' and 'Pacifics' on main-line trains, while the

freights were handled by various NER and 'J39' 0-6-0s , a 'B16' 4-6-0, 'V2s' and a couple of Ivatt Class 4 2-6-0s.

Our first 'new ground' soon came in the course of a journey in one of the elderly NER electric trains on the 20-mile circular trip via Jesmond, Monkseaton, Tynemouth and Wallsend. The scenery was unattractive, with suburbs giving way to flat coastal landscapes outward bound, in turn changing to scenes of heavy industry, following the north bank of the Tyne. Several of the more important intermediate stations showed the NER characteristic of providing imposing buildings with a large circulating area at the rear of the platforms. The car sheds were seen at South Gosforth, and we saw examples in service of the articulated units and the single parcel cars, as well as the more conventional sets. Numerous examples of the old NER slotted signal posts were noted.

Outside the works of Robert Stephenson & Co, alongside the Central station, was a large green 0-6-0ST numbered 81, one of two built for Richard Thomas & Baldwin of Ebbw Vale.

We continued our travels on the 10.30am express to Carlisle, 'V2' No 60818 with a light load of about six corridors including a buffet car. The allowance of 92 minutes for 60¼ miles with stops at Hexham and Haltwhistle appears generous, but nevertheless we enjoyed some fast running down into Carlisle.

After passing Blaydon sheds and yard the

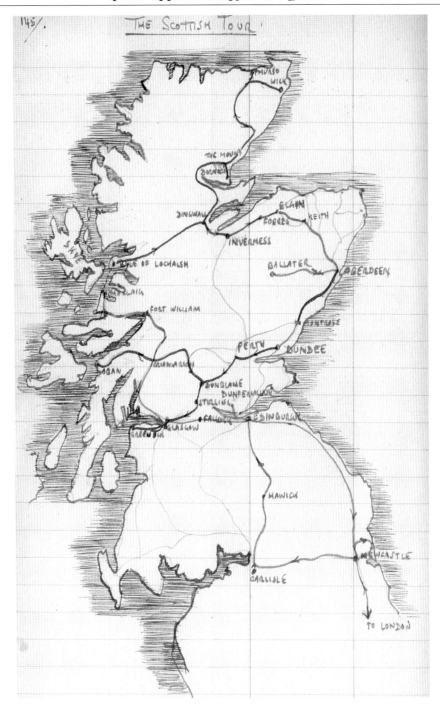

145.

THE SCOTTISH TOUR

scenery becomes quite picturesque as the railway follows the valley of the Tyne to Hexham, and thence the South Tyne to Haltwhistle, marred only by an occasional colliery in the early stages. At Blaydon BEA 0-4-0ST No 20 was seen, and another, NCB No 8 (*Acomb Unit*) at Bardon Mill. There is a small shed at Hexham, used by the Reedsmouth branch 'G5s' – we saw No 67320 on the connecting train.

A brief spell of observation at Carlisle was followed by a journey to Edinburgh on the 1.26pm Waverley Route express, on which an 'A1' had a chance to show its paces on an eight-coach train. The schedule allows 2hr 58min for the 98¼ miles with nine intermediate stops, those at Hawick and Galashiels being allowed 6 and 4 minutes respectively. The gradients are very hard in places, and there are two summits, at Whitrope (970 feet) and Falahill (880 feet), the former being approached by a 10-mile pull mostly at 1 in 75. Following the 10-mile descent to Hawick are 19 undulating miles to Galashiels and then the 15-mile climb to Falahill between 1 in 100 and 1 in 75. Thence to Edinburgh is almost entirely downhill, including over 8 miles at 1 in 70.

We suffered a long delay on the border bridge just after Kershope Foot station, and a fairly lengthy stop at Hawick left us about 10 minutes lost time to regain. This was easily accomplished.

Leaving Carlisle the line runs roughly NNE to Riccarton Junction, where it is joined by the line from Hexham through Reedsmouth. In this isolated spot, accessible only by railway, there is an Engineers' Department depot and a loco coaling station. One engine, 'C15' 4-4-2T No 67477, is in store here. After Riccarton, a northerly course is taken through Hawick to St Boswells, where lines from Berwick and Tweedmouth are joined. There is a locomotive depot at Hawick where about 30 engines, almost entirely NBR in origin, are stabled. There are smaller depots, each two-road buildings, at St Boswells and Galashiels. Leaving St Boswells the line swings almost due east through Melrose to Galashiels, where an alternative route to Edinburgh , via Peebles, branches off. Heading due north-east from Galashiels, after topping Falahill summit a descent is made to the colliery-scarred Lothian plain, and the East Coast main line is joined at Portobello.

'Pacifics' of Classes 'A1' and 'A3' from Haymarket and Carlisle (Canal) work the principal trains, 4-4-0s of Class 'D49' and of NB classes, and 'B1' Class 4-6-0s also participate. The freights are largely worked by St Margarets 'K3s', with NB 0-6-0s from Hawick on local work.

In the evening we visited Dalry Road shed (64C) where 29 engines were recorded, including 'Compounds', Class 5s, Horwich 2-6-0s, Stanier 2-6-4Ts, Caledonian 0-6-0s, 0-6-0Ts and 0-4-4Ts, and one or two NBR engines. Three 'visitors' were noted, Nos 44921 (68A), 45484 (66A) and 64527 (65E).

15 May 1945: Ex-NBR 'J37' 0-6-0 No 64543 basks in the sunshine outside Edinburgh Seafield shed, the most important of St Margarets' several outstations.

15 May 1945: What would have been unthinkable in pre-Grouping days is the sight of a 'North British' loco on a 'Caley' shed! Now, under BR management, 'J37' 0-6-0 No 64591 rests happily at Dalry Road.

We then visited the sub-depots to St Margarets at South Leith and Seafield, situated alongside each other on the shore of the Firth of Forth. The former consists simply of a siding used by NBR 0-6-2Ts, 0-6-0Ts and 0-4-0Ts, which shunt the adjacent goods yards. The latter, somewhat more pretentious, consists of a two-road shed with coal ramp, and houses mainly 0-6-0s.

## SUNDAY 16 MAY 1954

Sunday was devoted mainly to shed visits, and the rail journeys were purely incidental. Leaving Waverley on the 11.22am train to Dunfermline Lower, calling at Haymarket and Inverkeithing, our 'V1' 2-6-2T treated us to some sprightly running between Haymarket and the approaches to the Forth Bridge, with a train consisting of about eight well-filled compartment coaches. After a prolonged halt at Inverkeithing we climbed steadily to Dunfermline, entering the station after traversing a high viaduct.

Thence to Stirling our travels were by bus, with frequent views of the riverside loop line between Dunfermline and Alloa via Kincardine.

From Stirling we caught the 4.24pm train, a Perth-Glasgow (Queen Street) express, hauled by No 45214 and calling at Larbert only. The route taken involved transferring from the Stirling-Buchanan Street to the Queen Street route at Bonnybridge. A Kittybrewster 'B1', No 61403, presumably ex-Cowlairs Works,

was shunting at Bishopbriggs and Nos 61344 (65A), 61754, 61219 (68E), 67619 (65C), 42738 (63C) and 90771 (66B) were in the works yard at Cowlairs.

A brief summary of the shed visits follows:

**St Margarets (64A):** There were 130 engines on shed, out of an allocation of around 200, of which a number are 'subbed' at Dunbar, Galashiels, Polton, Penicuik, North Berwick, Longniddry, Seafield and South Leith, while others spend the Sunday on the Craigentinny loop. The shed, situated a mile or so east of Waverley station, consists of a long six-road building with a cramped yard alongside, and a turntable on the opposite side of the main lines around which most of the 0-4-0 and 0-6-0 tanks stand. The allocation includes several 'V2s', a dozen 'B1s' and a large array of 'K3s', to which are entrusted fast freight work along the Anglo-Scottish main line. Numerous Gresley 2-6-2Ts and an assortment of NB and 'Shire' Class 4-4-0s work local passenger traffic, and no fewer than 65 0-6-0s of Classes 'J35', 'J36', 'J37', 'J38' and 'J39' perform freight duties, together with about a dozen 'M of S' 2-8-0s. An army of shunting tanks includes numerous 'N15' Class 0-6-2s, 'J83' and 'J88' Class 0-6-0s, and 'Y9' 0-4-0 'Pugs'.

Visitors at the time of our inspection included Nos 60516 (52A), 60835 (52B) and 61851 (68E). Two LMR Ivatt 2MT 2-6-0s, Nos 46461/62, are stationed here, both of these being on shed.

*Above* 16 May 1954: At St Margarets shed ex-NBR 'D34' No 62487 *Glen Arklet* has a 'V1' 2-6-2T for company.

*Below* 16 May 1954: Two of St Margarets shed's fleet of shunters pose by the turntable. On the left is Class 'Y9' 0-4-0ST No 68099, with 'J83' 0-6-0ST No 68463 as stablemate.

31

*Above* 16 May 1954: Dunfermline shed is host to 'D30' 4-4-0 No 62427 *Dumbiedykes* (a character from one of Sir Walter Scott's novels).

*Below* 16 May 1954: Class 'J36' 0-6-0 No 65320, an ex-NBR veteran of 1899 construction, is coaled up ready for its next duty at Dunfermline shed.

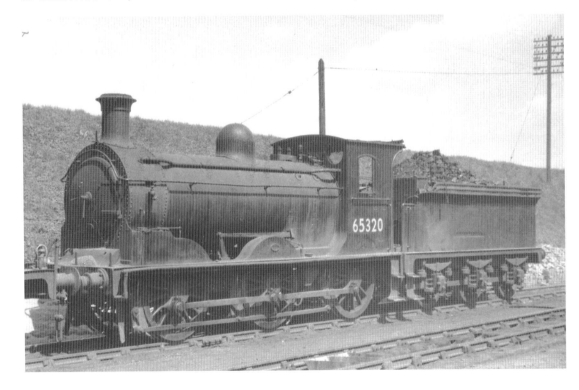

**Haymarket (64B):** The majority of the Haymarket roster of 80 engines are passenger tender types, including 'Pacifics' of Classes 'A1', 'A2', 'A3' and 'A4', and 4-4-0s of Classes 'D11', 'D30' and 'D49', with several mixed-traffic 'B1s' and 'V2s'. The few tank engines include 'V1s', 'J83s', 'J88s' and a couple of 'N15s'.

'Pacifics' from Newcastle and Carlisle are of course regular visitors, while a variety of engines use the extensive repair shops alongside the shed, which contained an LMR 2-6-4T, No 42272, and a Bathgate 'N15', No 69158, among others at the time of our visit.

**Dunfermline (62C):** Strategically situated north of the Forth Bridge at the junction of several routes carrying heavy industrial traffic, Dunfermline is predominantly a freight depot, a handful of NB 4-4-0s and 4-4-2Ts and a couple of 2-6-2Ts being the only passenger engines out of the 75 or so stabled here.

**Stirling (63B):** The LMR shed is a rather tumbledown four-road depot alongside the main line, handling about 30 engines of which a dozen are CR 2F 0-6-0s, and there are several 0-4-4Ts and 0-6-0Ts of pre-Grouping CR origin. Standard engines include a few Stanier '5s' and 4F 0-6-0s, and a couple of 2-6-4Ts. There were 33 engines on shed, including Nos 45156, 45355 (65B), 44978 (63A) and 44331 (63E).

The ER depot, a small two-road affair, provides motive power for the routes to Alloa and Dumbarton. There were ten engines on shed, Nos 54489, 62714/25, 64501/42/44/69, 64946 (64A) and 67650/75.

**Eastfield (65A):** It is only a year since this great depot, stabling about 150 engines, was last visited, but in view of the wide variety of locomotives it is probably one of the most interesting in Scotland. Here can be seen 'Pacifics' from Haymarket, 'B1s', 'K2s', 'K4s' and 'V4s' from the West Highland line, 'D11' and 'D30' 4-4-0s, 'J50', 'Q1' and 'V1' tanks of recent years, and 'N15s', 'J83s' and 'J88s' of the NB era, LMS Class 5s and Class 4 2-6-0s, and a fleet of NBR 0-6-0s. On shed awaiting or

ex-Cowlairs Works were 'J69' No 68562 (68B), 62418 (62A), 40572 (67B), 40670 (67C), 61720/24 (40B), 68351 (62C), 54469 (63A), 68322 (62A), 61352 (61A), 61737 (38A) and 67644 (62C).

**Parkhead (65C):** A late-evening visit recorded 57 engines including numerous 'V1s' and 'N2s'. Of the latter, Nos 69564/95 were in store, in very bad condition. A 'C15', No 67470, and 'C16' Nos 67482/7, 67500, a 'J72', 69015, 15 Class 'N15s' and GER 'J69' No 68503 were noted.

## MONDAY 17 MAY 1954

The morning trip from busy St Enoch terminus to Greenock reminded us of last year's trip to Gourock, as a further example of the energetic way in which these Clyde Coast residential services are handled. Our train, the 10.50am, consisted of five coaches worked by a Fairburn 2-6-4T, and with eight intermediate stops is allowed 57 minutes for the 26 miles, entailing an average running speed around 35mph. Some steady climbing is involved in both directions, as the line skirts the hills high above the Clyde from Kilmacolm, whence the 6½ miles down to Greenock (Lynedoch) are run in about 8 or 9 minutes. Away below, the shipyards can be seen, with the route via Port Glasgow and the sheds at Cartsdyke clearly visible.

On the outward journey the route taken from Shields Road was via Corkerhill and Paisley (Canal). Returning, we used the alternate line via Paisley (Gilmour Street) and Ibrox, the two routes dividing at Elderslie. 4-4-0 No 54498 was motive power on the up run. At Greenock Princes Pier the shed was visited, ten engines being noted, including 4-4-0 Nos 41149, 54479/92 and 54506/08.

A complete circuit was made of the Glasgow Underground. There are 14 stations, practically identical in design, each with an island platform for the two-car trains. The older stock have 'gates' like the early London tube carriages, but some vehicles are fitted with automatic doors. An outside third rail is used for current collection, and contact is made with a continuous bar at about window height for signalling purposes.

In the afternoon we left Queen Street on the 3.46pm to Fort William, about six coaches headed by 'B1' No 61396. Departure was delayed by 35 minutes waiting for the connection from London, but 20 minutes were regained by smart running throughout the route, particularly on the comparatively level stretch between the junction alongside Eastfield shed and Craigendoran. This section carries a fairly respectable suburban service along the north bank of the River Clyde, connection being made at Dumbarton with the LMS & LNER joint branch to Balloch and the ex-LNER route from Stirling. At Craigendoran there is a short branch to Helensburgh (Lower), and the West Highland line begins in earnest with a sharp 3-mile climb alongside the Gare Loch, followed by a gentle descent of 5 miles to Garelochhead. These sheltered waters were used during the war as a naval base and a branch was laid to Faslane serving Military Port No 1. Even now we could see three 'KGV' battleships (almost certainly including *Duke of York* and *Anson*, scrapped at Faslane), two aircraft carriers and two cruisers, some of the ships obviously stripped of guns and completely out of service.

From Garelochhead is a 6-mile climb, partly at 1 in 54, to the summit just beyond Glen Douglas, then a 3-mile descent at 1 in 57 to Arrochar & Tarbet on the shores of Loch Lomond. Another 8 miles of gentle downgrade brought us to Ardlui, at the northern end of the loch, then follow 8 gruelling miles, mostly at 1 in 60, to Crianlarich, where the Oban line is crossed, the two routes being linked by a double-track connection laid during recent years. Crianlarich, like most other stations on the West Highland line, consists of an island platform. After a short descent, 6 more miles follow at 1 in 60 to a summit a mile beyond Tyndrum. The next 6 miles descend equally sharply to Bridge of Orchy, after which the next 8 miles are against the collar to Gorton, followed by 6 miles descending rather less sharply, before the final climb, 8 miles long, is encountered from Rannoch to Corrour. At Rannoch the scenery is particularly wild and desolate, as the moor of that name is crossed, with views of Loch Laidon.

From Corrour the remaining 28 miles are practically all downhill, with Loch Treig to the west of the line from Corrour to Tulloch. At the latter the line bends sharply and runs due west to Spean Bridge, where the now disused Fort Augustus branch runs in from the north alongside Loch Lochy. Thence we turn south-west to Fort William, joining the Mallaig extension at Mallaig Junction, 1 mile outside the station.

Fort William is a terminal with two platforms, one of which is an island. Outside are goods sidings and, at right-angles to the line, a two-road engine shed.

We saw little traffic en route. At Shandon a train of hoppers of 'bulk aluminium' hauled by 'K4' No 61996 was passed, and we crossed the double-headed up train at Ardlui instead of Crianlarich. Throughout, the scenery is magnificent – unsurpassable, I suggest, anywhere in the British Isles. The summit at Corrour in 1,347 feet above sea level.

The current winter timetable shows two weekday trains leaving Glasgow at 5.46am and 3.46pm respectively, the former conveying sleeping cars from King's Cross. The two corresponding up trains leave Fort William at 9.28am and 2.52pm, having left Mallaig at 7.42am and 1.00pm. There is a third train in each direction between Fort William and Mallaig, down at 4.50pm and up at 6.35am.

Motive power consists of Classes 'K1', 'K2' and 'K4', 'B1', 'V4' and Class 5s, and Fort William shed has three or four 'K2s', two 'K4s' and three 'J36s' for local freight and ballast work. In addition, three or four 'K2s' are kept at Mallaig.

In the evening we visited the shed, and recorded Nos 45214, 61775/83, 62011, 61134, 61995, 65237 and 65300/13.

## TUESDAY 18 MAY 1954

'K2s' Nos 61775/86 arrived about 30 minutes late from Glasgow, and we left Fort William behind 'K1' No 62034 with three coaches and

18 May 1954: The shed at Kyle of Lochalsh, with a 'Black Five' lurking inside, is typical of the smaller Highland Railway structures.

three vans at 10.50am. We lost 4 minutes more en route and arrived at Mallaig at 12.30pm. Once again the scenery was superb, with glorious views of the snow-streaked face of Ben Nevis as we forged along the level from Banavie, where the Caledonian Canal is crossed on a swing bridge, westwards along Locheilside.

This section of the West Highland is a far less tough proposition from the locomotive point of view, and gradients, though as sharp as 1 in 48 in places, are short and undulating. A fine view is obtained of the head of Loch Sheil at Glenfinnan, then the coast is reached at Beasdale and the line turns north at Arisaig to drop down through Morar to Mallaig. Perhaps the best-known engineering feature of the whole line is the concrete Glenfinnan Viaduct, 416 yards long and 100 feet high on a 12-chain curve, with 21 arched spans.

At Mallaig our train was met by the boat that was to take us on the 2¼-hour trip to the Kyle of Lochalsh, and we disembarked at the end of our short voyage at about 3pm. The Kyle station consists of an island platform on the jetty, with adjacent sidings. The two-road locomotive shed, a stone building with an ex-LNWR carriage body alongside, is a short distance inland.

The Kyle branch leaves the Highland main line from Inverness to Wick and Thurso at Dingwall, and is 63 miles long. It was opened as far as Strome Ferry, a few miles short of the present terminus, in 1870, and the remainder was opened to traffic in 1897. It is single track throughout, with 13 intermediate stations and halts, most of the former having passing loops, and the current winter timetable provides for two down and three up trains. Both down trains are through from Inverness, but only one of the up trains runs through, the others making connections at Dingwall with trains from the north. One train each way conveys a restaurant car between Inverness and Achnasheen.

From Dingwall the line is level as far as Fodderty Junction (2½ miles), where the now closed branch to Strathpeffer diverges, then follows an almost unbroken climb of 4 miles at 1 in 50 to Ravens Rock summit (458 feet). Sharp undulations follow, then comes a 15-mile climb to Luib summit (646 feet), 4 miles west of Achnasheen, including a good proportion at 1 in 60 and 1 in 75, and a short stretch at 1 in 40. Thence the line falls almost continually to Strathcarron, and the remainder of the route is comparatively level save for a few undulations at 1 in 50 or 60.

At Lochluichart a deviation has been constructed to carry the line clear of the new water level that will result from the construction of a new dam. There are numerous bridges and viaducts along the route, and impressive rock cuttings between Strome Ferry and Kyle of Lochalsh.

We found Nos 44788 and 44799 on Kyle shed, with 0-4-4T No 55216 shunting, and left the Kyle at 5.35pm behind No 45361 with

18 May 1954: Class 5 4-6-0 No 45361 heads a Dingwall train at Kyle of Lochalsh, with the Isle of Skye as a backdrop.

three coaches. All passenger and freight work is now handled by Stanier '5s', and we passed No 45453 at Achnasheen with four coaches, an eight-wheeled and a four-wheeled van, on the 5.00pm from Inverness.

At Dingwall our train drew up at the outer edge of the up island platform, and the locomotive went on shed, to join 0-4-4T No 55199. We continued to Inverness on the 3.35pm from Wick (8.57pm ex-Dingwall), and backed into the terminal after running past the shed and Lochgorm Works. Outside the latter were Pickersgill 4-4-0 Nos 54472/80 and the last Highland Railway tender engine, 4-4-0 No 54398 *Ben Alder*, withdrawn in January 1953.

## WEDNESDAY 19 MAY 1954

We caught the 6.40am train from Inverness to the north, consisting of four coaches, one Pullman car and 4 bogie vans, headed by the inevitable Class 5, No 44718. As far as Dingwall we were on ground traversed the previous day, running quite fast as far as Beauly, with double track for a few miles after crossing the Caledonian Canal at Clachnaharry, just north of Inverness. At Muir of Ord Junction we had a glimpse of the Fortrose branch, closed to passenger traffic in October 1951, and then, after leaving Dingwall, kept close company with the Cromarty Firth as far as Invergordon, originating point of much heavy naval traffic during the 1914-18 war.

A few miles north of Invergordon the line makes one of the great detours that add so much mileage to the journey, curving from a north-westerly direction first north-east through Tain alongside the Dornoch Firth to Bonar Bridge, then north through Invershin and Culrain (only a quarter of a mile apart on opposite banks of the River Oykell), and then at Lairg due east to Rogart. Thence to The Mound the line is actually heading south-east before reaching the coast at Golspie an closely following the latter to Helmsdale.

There is a small shed at Tain, and we crossed the 6.25am up from Helmsdale here, headed by Nos 44723 and 45474. At Rogart we passed No 45478 on a freight train, and detrained at

*Above* 19 May 1954: The crew of this Inverness to Wick train watch while Class 5 No 44783 removes the restaurant car at The Mound.

*Below* 19 May 1954: This rare survivor arriving at The Mound is Highland Railway 0P 0-4-4T No 55053, on a mixed train from the Dornoch branch.

The Mound to await the arrival of the branch train from Dornoch. So far the scenery, though lacking the grandeur of the West Highland or Kyle lines, had been attractive in a rugged style. Later on, north of Helmsdale, we found over 40 miles of the most desolate and unattractive landscape in these islands, devoid of a single tree or shrub and supporting only a handful of widely separated communities deriving a livelihood from herds of sheep. In these isolated regions the line is bordered for miles by tumbledown snow-fences.

At The Mound our Pullman car had been shunted into a siding, to await the arrival of the 8.35am from Wick. The next train on the scene was a northbound freight headed by No 45361 piloted by 4-4-0 No 54495 (60C). The latter ran on light to Helmsdale while the former shunted in the tiny goods yard.

Eventually we sighted the Dornoch branch train puffing its way across the long causeway, and as it pulled into the branch platform, alongside and lower than the main-line platform, we found it to comprise a Brake 3rd corridor carriage and goods brake-van headed by ex-Highland Railway Peter Drummond 0P 0-4-4T No 55053.

No 44798 arrived on the up passenger train, and the Pullman was shunted onto the rear by the tank engine.

At 11.55am we left for Dornoch, the 7¾ miles being allowed 43 minutes with three intermediate stations. The branch is worked as a light railway, and frequent stops are made to open and shut crossing gates. For the last few miles the line heads due south. Dornoch station has a single platform with loop, three sidings and a small shed

After returning to The Mound we continued at 1.51pm on the 10.40am ex-Inverness, with engines Nos 44718/89. A buffet car next to the engine was removed at Helmsdale. We passed No 44784 on an up freight, and found the other 0P, No 55051, with CR 3F 0-6-0 No 57587 occupying the two-road shed. Our pilot came off, and we continued northwards across the wastelands unassisted, crossing the summit of 708 feet.

We detrained at Georgemas Junction, where 0-4-4T No 55236 was waiting for the Thurso portion of two coaches, detached from the rear of our train. No 44783 was heading the 3.35pm ex-Wick. We continued to Thurso, the most northerly station in the British Isles, consisting of one platform with a carriage road alongside, roofed over for a short distance. Adjacent is a goods yard and small engine shed.

Our rail travels were finished for the day, but we continued by bus to Wick, where we visited the engine shed, a substantial two-road stone structure with a small mechanical coaling-plant. CR 4-4-0 Nos 54459/91/96 were on shed with our Class 5.

19 May 1954: A long way from home! The shed at Wick, 690 miles from Euston, is host to ex-CR 3P 'Dunalastair IV' 4-4-0 No 54459 bearing express headlamps.

## THURSDAY 20 MAY 1954

With the exception of the 14¼ miles from Wick to Georgemas Junction, all of this day's travelling was on 'old ground', the Inverness-Aberdeen route having been covered in October 1947.

We travelled south on the morning train, 8.35am ex-Wick, one of the two daily trains north of Helmsdale. One of the CR 4-4-0s, No 54491, was on ballast duties at Altnabreac, as were Nos 57587 and 44788 at Rogart. Another 4-4-0, No 54487, was seen on a freight train at Invergordon.

During a 1½-hour break at Inverness we visited the shed, and found the famous roundhouse occupied by a dozen or so Class 5s, one or two CR 4-4-0s, 0-6-0s and tank engines. 'Pug' tank No 56038 (65D) was acting as Lochgorm Works pilot, and 0-4-4T No 55231 (62B) was shunting around the station.

The 4.00pm to Aberdeen, three LNER coaches, two vans and through coaches for Aviemore had No 44798 as motive power as far as Cairnie Junction, between Keith and Huntly. During a 14-minute stop at Forres, junction with the original main line to the south, a brief visit was paid to the shed, occupied by two very clean 4-4-0s, Nos 54473/82. Here our through carriages for Aviemore were detached.

At Elgin the GNSR terminus is adjacent to the HR through station, and two alternative routes to Aberdeen diverge here, connection being made with trains serving both routes. One route follows the coast through Buckie, turning southwards through Tillynaught, junction for the Banff branch, and rejoining the main line at Cairnie Junction, beyond Keith. The other route is to the south of the HR line, through Craigellachie, junction for Boat of Garten and Dufftown, and links up again with the HR line at Keith.

Our train waited an hour at Keith, and shortly before departure time 'B1' No 61352 arrived from Elgin via Craigellachie, and the carriages were added to our train. At Cairnie Junction, an island platform in the wilderness, we awaited the arrival of 'B1' No 61324 with two coaches from Elgin via Buckie. Our Class 5 came off here and returned light towards Keith, while the 'B1' backed on with its carriages to form a train for Aberdeen with portions from three distinct routes!

During our wait at Keith we visited the four-road shed, last home of most of the GNSR 'D40' Class 4-4-0s. We noted Nos 62262/68/71/73/74/75 on shed or around the yards, with 'D34' No 62882, 'K2' No 61729 (61A) and 2P No 40603 (61A).

Another 'K2', No 61792, was passed at Huntly on a westbound passenger train (6.10pm Aberdeen-Keith), followed at Gartly by No 61348 on the 6.50pm express from Aberdeen. The main line from Keith to Aberdeen is double throughout.

At Inveramsay the long branch to Macduff, closed in September 1951, joins the main line, and at Inverurie is another closed branch, to Old Meldrum. A glimpse of engines in the works yard showed various 4-4-0s and 0-6-0s. Passing Kittybrewster we saw 'J37' No 64622 (65A), ex-works.

## FRIDAY 21 MAY 1954

A morning trip on the Deeside branch to Ballater preceded our shed visits and main-line travels, leaving Aberdeen Joint station on the first down train of the day, the 8.11am, comprising three coaches hauled by 'B1' No 61308 fitted with a wedge-shaped snowplough. There are three trains in each direction on weekdays only, the first down and last up stopping at all stations, the second down and first up missing Cambus O'May Halt, and the 6.05pm down and 10.20am up being non-stop between Aberdeen and Banchory (17 miles). Journey time is between 80 and 98 minutes for the 43¼ miles. The branch leaves the main line to the south at Ferryhill Junction, and is single throughout. The scenery becomes increasingly rugged and attractive, and in many cases evidence was seen of the great damage caused to forests by the gales of early 1953.

Banchory is the most important intermediate station, and in adjacent sidings here and

*Above* 21 May 1954: Ballater station had its moments of glory when the Royal Family were en route to and from Balmoral, but all is peaceful there as 'B1' No 61308 is about to leave for Aberdeen.

*Below* 21 May 1954: Aberdeen Kittybrewster was the main depot for the Great North of Scotland Railway, but it is ex-NBR 'D34' 4-4-0 No 62493 *Glen Loy* that we see on the turntable.

elsewhere along the branch are stored a great variety of passenger vehicles awaiting or ex-Inverurie works.

The terminus at Ballater consists of one lengthy platform, with nearby goods yard and locomotive shed, occupied at the time of our visit by a 'K2' 2-6-0. The morning up train, passed at Culter, was hauled by No 80005, and on the return journey we crossed No 90041 on a freight at Park.

**Kittybrewster (61A):** About 10 of the 70 engines stationed here are subbed at Ballater, Macduff, Fraserburgh and Peterhead, but accommodation in the old roundhouse is by no means ample for the remainder, as numerous engines on their way to or from Inverurie Works spend time here.

Practically all important passenger work on the GNS section is now entrusted to 'B1s', of which Kittybrewster has 16, reinforced by several BR Standard 2-6-4Ts. The unrebuilt 'B12s', which have been so prominent since the 'Sandringhams' displaced them from the GE section in the '20s, have now almost disappeared from the scene, and only one, No 61539, was on shed. Secondary work is still performed by GNS 'D40' Class 4-4-0s, now mainly concentrated on Keith shed, with a few NB and LMS standard 2P 4-4-0s – only one 'D40', No 62269, was seen, with NB Nos 62469/80/93 (Class 'D34') and 2P Nos 40600/650. The Fraserburgh-St Combs service

is now performed by an Ivatt Class 2 2-6-0, and the GER 'F4' it has displaced, No 67157, was rusting inside the shed, complete with 'cowcatcher'. Three of the GNS 0-4-2Ts, Nos 68191/2/3, were on shed. The fourth, No 68190, we saw later shunting on the quays. Engines for works included Nos 65234 (64F), 57295 (67C) and the following Ferryhill engines were also on shed: Nos 60531, 67455/96, 67501 and 65247. Shunting in the goods yards alongside the shed is largely in the hands of NER 'J72' tanks, Nos 68700/19/49/50 being seen.

**Ferryhill (61B):** This 12-road 'joint' shed is the home of big engines, with 'Pacifics', 'V2s' and 'M of S' 2-8-0s in the majority. Of 30 engines recorded, seven were 2-8-0s, five were 'V2s', two were 'A2' and one 'Duchess' 4-6-2s, and five were Stanier Class 5s. An interesting visitor for Inverurie Works was 'N2' No 69514 (65C), the second of the class to be shopped at Inverurie. 'Compound' No 41176 was in store, and to compensate for the Ferryhill engines on Kittybrewster shed, several 61A engines were noted.

Walking along the river bank we saw steeple-cabbed English Electric Co battery loco 'Registered by the Railway Executive No 261' working a train of coal wagons to the power station.

We left Aberdeen on the 3.40pm Edinburgh express, 'V2' No 60931 with 10 coaches. This

21 May 1954: One of the very few tank engines of GNSR origin that passed into BR ownership is 'Z5' 0-4-2T No 68193, seen at Kittybrewster shed.

train calls at Stonehaven. Montrose, Arbroath and Broughty Ferry, and we experienced great difficulty in starting from Stonehaven, justifying some very smart running to regain time. Just north of Montrose is Kinnaber Junction, where the LMS route to Perth and the south leaves the LNER route to Dundee, scene of exciting moments in the 'Race to Aberdeen', when the first train past Kinnaber won the day. From Montrose to Usan signal box, along a causeway, we traversed the only 2 miles of single track between King's Cross and Aberdeen. At Arbroath, junction is made with a branch from Forfar, and three engines are maintained at a small shed. Nos 55193 and 46464 were noted.

**Dundee (62B):** These are really two separate sheds, the LNER shed between the LNER and LMS main lines, and the somewhat larger LMS shed on the opposite side of the LMS tracks. The latter appears to be used for storage and light repairs, and 30 engines were housed in the eight-road brick building. The allocation includes a very good variety, the LMS roster comprising a Class 5 and a number of CR 0-6-0s, 0-4-4Ts and 0-6-0Ts and two Class 2 2-6-0s, and the LNER engines including two 'A2s', ten

21 May 1954: Prior to nationalisation, Dundee was served by both the LMS and the LNER, and both are represented here by ex-CR 2P 0-4-4T No 55223 and ex-LNER 'J38' 0-6-0 No 65924.

'V2s', some 'B1s', 'D34s' and 'D49s', numerous 0-6-0s of Classes 'J35', 'J36', 'J37', 'J38' and 'J39', 'C15' and 'C16' 4-4-2Ts, 'J83' 0-6-0Ts, 'Y9' 0-4-0Ts and 'M of S' 2-8-0s. An interesting service vehicle stationed here is mobile crane RS 1033.

The journey to Perth was made on the 7.10pm non-stop express, allowed 30 minutes for the 21¼ miles. Our Class 5 with a light load of five or six coaches, was brought to a halt on the outskirts of Perth in about 22 minutes, after a very fast sustained run, before crawling slowly into the sharply curved platforms alongside the main station.

**Perth (63A):** Some 120 engines are stationed at this very important junction, from which lines radiate to Inverness and the north, Dundee, Aberdeen via Forfar, Glasgow via Stirling, Alloa and Dunfermline via Kinross Junction, and to Ladybank (closed to passenger traffic). The only LNER engines stationed at 63A are a couple of 'Shires', but we noted 'A2' No 60536, 'D34' Nos 62470/84, 'D30' No 62426 and 'B1' Nos 61102/08. At the station 'A3' No 60035, 'B1' No 61278 (62B) and 'D49' No 62744 were all at the head of passenger trains.

The LMS types include a number of 'Compounds' (of which we noted Nos 40921/23 out of use at the back of the shed), some 4F 0-6-0s, numerous Pickersgill 4-4-0s (of which five are 'subbed' at Blair Atholl for banking duties), CR

0-4-4Ts and 0-6-0Ts, and a few CR 0-6-0s. By far the most numerous individual class, however, responsible for all passenger work north of Perth and a great proportion of trains to the south, are the Stanier '5s', of which there are about 60, probably the most at any shed in the country. These have been supplemented by a few of the Standard BR variety.

The following visitors were recorded: Nos 61278 (62B), 55215 (63E), 43884 (63B), 42837, 72007/8 (68A), 61102 (62B), 45718 (68A), 46242 and 55262 (67C).

## SATURDAY 22 MAY 1954

Leaving Perth at 7.50am on a southbound stopping train headed by one of the BR 'Standard 5s', we changed at Dunblane onto a Glasgow-Oban Train, the 8.00am from Buchanan Street, which arrived about 20 minutes late behind No 45463. At Gleneagles, between Perth and Dunblane, we connected with a train from Comrie, worked by 4F No 44258. This line extends beyond Comrie along the north bank of Loch Earn to join the Callander & Oban route at Balquhidder, but there are no passenger services west of Comrie. Another line, closed in 1951, leaves the Inverness and Aberdeen main lines at Almond Valley Junction, fast north of Perth, and joins the Gleneagles-Comrie line at Crieff.

The Callander & Oban line is 82 miles long from the junction at Dunblane, and was opened in 1880. Penetrating mountainous country and skirting various lochs, it is a rival scenically to the West Highland line, and is single track from Doune, the first station out of Dunblane, with a ruling gradient of 1 in 50. Apart from the Gleneagles-Balquhidder route already mentioned, there is a short branch from Killin Junction to Killin, and a 28-mile-long branch from Connel Ferry, 6 miles short of Oban, to Ballachulish, at the head of the Pass of Glencoe. The West Highland Line passes overhead at Crianlarich, and there is a connection between the two routes used by freight trains and by a daily summer service from Glasgow (Queen Street) to Oban.

The winter timetable shows five down and

four up trains, the discrepancy being due to the limitation to six coaches unassisted westbound compared with eight coaches eastbound, for Class 5 4-6-0s. There are one or two services from Oban to Ballachulish, reversing at Connel Ferry, and several services between Stirling and Callander. The Killin branch has five trains each way, and the Ballachulish branch four trains.

From Balquhidder the line climbs to the 940-foot summit at Glenoglehead, with a splendid view of Loch Earn below, and then drops at 1 in 69 to Killin Junction. For some distance onwards gradients are comparatively easy, through Crianlarich and up Strathfillan with the West Highland line at a higher level on the other side of the valley. The gradient becomes stiffer before Tyndrum, and the start from that station is at 1 in 49, but the line then drops to Dalmally, crosses the River Orchy, and emerges alongside Loch Awe. Beyond the loch the Pass of Brander is reached, where a wire fence is linked to 14 signal posts to give warning of rock falls. A train was derailed here by a large boulder in 1946.

We had seen CR 0-6-0 No 57257 shunting at Callander, and another, 57460, on the Killin branch train. Class 5 No 45159 was passed at Luib, on a freight train, and No 44956 at Crianlarich on the connecting spur, while No 45154 was working the 9.12am ex-Oban. On arrival at Connel Ferry, where we used the outer edge of the island platform, 0-4-4T No 55208 was in charge of the two-coach branch train. Leaving the station we had a good view of the cantilever viaduct carrying the Ballachulish branch over Loch Etive, and we then climbed at 1 in 50 to Glencruitten summit, where the signal box, perched above the line, forms the lower storey of a house.

The line then descends steeply into Oban, making a very sharp curve round the outskirts of the town, into the spacious four-platform terminus on the quayside.

On visiting the shed we recorded Nos 44786, 44880, 45448, 55195, 55263, 57254 and 57424.

We left Oban for Glasgow on the 4.45pm train, passing No 45117 at Dalmally and No 44957 at Balquhidder. An unusual gradient post at Killin Junction shows grades of '1 in 50⅓' and '1 in 718¼'. Our train divided at Stirling into

*Above* 22 May 1954: A steamy scene at Oban shed, with ex-CR 2F 0-6-0 No 57424 hemmed in by a couple of 'Black Fives'.

*Left* 23 May 1954: Grangemouth's allocation was 'all ex-LMS' with just one exception, ex-NBR 'C15' 4-4-2T No 67480.

*Left* 23 May 1954: Twenty-one years after the Grouping, every loco on view at Polmont shed is of NBR origin. Prominent are 'little and large' 0-6-0s of Classes 'J36' and 'J37' respectively.

Glasgow and Edinburgh portions, the Glasgow portion calling at Larbert and Greenhill, arriving at Buchanan Street at 9.00pm.

## SUNDAY 23 MAY 1954

Once again Sunday was occupied mainly in shed visits, and our only rail travelling was along the only route open between Edinburgh and Glasgow on Sundays, the main LNER line via Falkirk. To the latter town we travelled on the 11.00am express hauled by an 'A3' 'Pacific' with an eight-coach train. We set back onto the wrong line at Eastfield, but made up some of the lost time before reaching Falkirk.

Continuing from Falkirk on the 6.37pm, we had a 'B1', stopping at Haymarket only.

**Polmadie (60A):** We visited this shed before leaving Glasgow, where 133 engines were recorded. They comprised the usual selection, Stanier, Fairburn and Standard BR 2-6-4Ts, 'Princess' and 'Duchess' 'Pacifics', 'Royal Scots' and 'Jubilees', Class 5s, 4F 0-6-0s, 'Jinties', and various types of CR 0-6-0s, 0-6-0Ts and 0-4-4Ts, 'Compounds'. McIntosh and Pickersgill 4-4-0s, 'M of S' 2-8-0s and 2-10-0s. Strangers included Nos 40177 (65D), 42882 (68A), 46152 (8A), 45712 (26A), 46201 (8A) and 57690 (66D).

**Grangemouth (65F):** This six-road depot maintains about 36 engines, all of freight or mixed-traffic types excepting two or three CR 0-4-4Ts. CR tank and tender engines are in the majority, but several 'M of S' 2-10-0s are stationed here, with a few Class 5s, 4F 0-6-0s and two Horwich 2-6-0s. Two NBR 4-4-2Ts, Nos 67454/80 (65C), were in store.

**Polmont (54C):** Of over 40 engines, the only post-Grouping types allocated to Polmont are a pair of Ivatt 4MT 2-6-0s, Nos 43140/41, and two 'J38s', Nos 65909/17). Apart from these and two GER 'J69s', Nos 68524/44, the remainder are all NBR engines of classes 'N15', 'C15/16', 'J88' and 'Y9'. There were 37 engines on shed, the building being a wooden structure of the 'through' type.

**Bathgate (64F):** This is being rebuilt, and almost all the engines were in the open. Like Polmont, post-1923 influence is hardly felt here – in fact, the whole allocation consists of NBR engines, and only one 'visitor', 'K2' No 61722, spoiled the 'illusion'. The small 'J36' 0-6-0s are in the majority here – 17 out of 35 locos on shed were of this type. The only tanks are 'N15' 0-6-2s, but one Polmont 4-4-2T, No 67473, was noted. There are a couple of 4-4-0s here, 'D30' No 62439, and 'D34' No 62495.

## MONDAY 24 MAY 1954

The 10.00am 'Flying Scotsman' gave us a good run home, with an arrival at King's Cross a few minutes before the scheduled time of 5.45pm. We had an 'A4' to Newcastle, 'A1' No 60150 from Newcastle to Grantham, and 'A4' No 60022 to King's Cross. A 'C16', No 67497, was noted in store at Longniddry, and NCB 0-6-0ST No 25 at Cramlington. Among the numerous engines recorded at York was No 73045 (10C). At Potters Bar a PW slack is in force in connection with the widening of the bottleneck through the station and tunnels. Work on the new station and goods yard is already well advanced.

A diesel shunter was seen in New England yard, one of a number newly allocated there.

| Summary of the Scottish tour, 15-24 May 1954 | | | | | |
|---|---|---|---|---|---|
| | LMS | LNER | WD | BR | Total |
| Locos booked | 158 | 343 | 20 | 7 | 528 |
| Mileage | 780½ | 1,269¾ | | | 2,050¼ |
| New mileage* | 369¼ | 380 | | | 749¼ |
| * Excluding Glasgow Underground | | | | | |

# NORTH WALES AND THE ISLE OF MAN

*T*his was a holiday with my parents, based on Llandudno, but they *happily accepted my suggestion for the railway outings, not least because one was a trip up Snowdon on the rack railway. That was on a rather dismal day, but fortunately it was calm and bright for our 'cruise' to the Isle of Man, on the small steamer St Tudno. Although a rather grumpy official refused to let me into the shed at Douglas, I came away a lifelong devotee of the 'narrow gauge'.*

**D**uring the course of a week based on Llandudno, a number of journeys were made covering the whole of the Chester & Holyhead main line of the former LNWR together with branches from it, and that section of the former Cambrian Railways between Corwen and Afon Wen via Barmouth Junction. Before describing in detail the journeys in Wales and to and from London, a few notes on the Chester & Holyhead line are given.

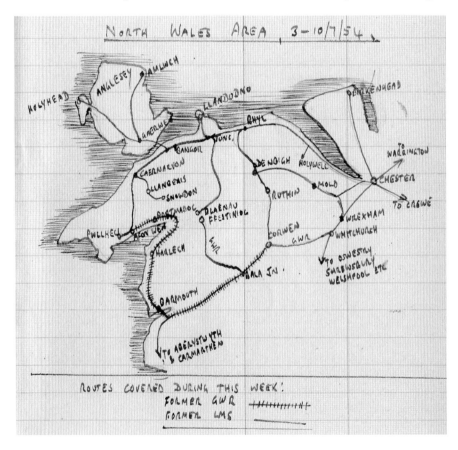

July 1954: Open-topped Llandudno & Colwyn Bay tramcar No 11 (ex-Bournemouth Corporation) at Craig-y-don.

This route, a continuation of that leaving the LNWR Anglo-Scottish main line at Crewe, is 84½ miles long, double track throughout, with considerable quadruple stretches between Chester and Llandudno Junction. The estuary of the Dee and the North Wales coast are closely followed for most of the route, the Menai Straits being crossed by means of a tubular bridge designed by Robert Stephenson. Travelling westwards from Chester, the LMS/GWR joint line to Birkenhead diverges immediately outside the General station, soon followed by a junction with the GWR route to London via Shrewsbury, and at Saltney Ferry the route to Denbigh via Mold branches off to the south-west. Other branches leave the main line at Holywell Junction for Holywell Town, Rhyl for Corwen via Denbigh, Llandudno Junction for Llandudno to the north and Blaenau Ffestiniog to the south, Bangor for Bethesda (closed to traffic), Menai Bridge for Afon Wen and Llanberis, and Gaerwen for Amlwch.

On the whole, gradients are very easy, being almost non-existent from Chester to Colwyn Bay and with minor undulations from there onwards, particularly on the Isle of Anglesey, as steep as 1 in 100 in places. This is not true of the branches. As an extreme, the 1½-mile Holywell Town branch is pitched at 1 in 27 almost the whole way, while the Blaenau Ffestiniog branch, after Bettws-y-Coed, rises continuously for 11 miles, part of which is at 1 in 47. The Amlwch branch undulates severely

throughout, and the Menai Bridge-Afon Wen line has a formidable climb in each direction to a summit near Pantglas, with a ruling gradient for down trains of 1 in 49

Traffic handled is considerable, particularly in the summer months when a constant procession of trains link the coastal resorts from Prestatyn to Llandudno with London, the Midlands and the North, in addition to the day and night Irish Mail services and through trains to and from Afon Wen. There are locomotive depots at Chester (6A), Mold Junction (6B), Rhyl (6K), with a sub-depot at Denbigh, Llandudno Junction (6G), Bangor (6H) and Holyhead (6J). Most of the freight motive power is concentrated at Mold Junction, though there are 0-6-0s at Rhyl, Llandudno Junction and Bangor, while apart from the dock shunting tanks Holyhead's allocation consists entirely of passenger and mixed-traffic engines.

The Irish Mail services are worked by 'Rebuilt Scots' now being supplemented by the latest batch of 'Britannia' 4-6-2s. Most of the other main-line passenger work is in the hands of Stanier and BR Class 5 4-6-0s, though a few 'Jubilees' or unrebuilt 'Patriots' can always be seen.

Local work is in the hands of 'Compound' and 2P 4-4-0s and 4P 2-6-4Ts on the main lines, and 3P and 2P 2-6-2Ts on the branches. 4F and L&Y 0-6-0s perform much of the local freight work, with 'WD' and 8F 2-8-0s on main-line turns. There are about 185 engines in all stationed at the sheds along the route.

## SATURDAY 3 JULY 1954

From St Pancras to Derby the 10.15am express was used, an 11-coach Manchester train calling at Kettering and Loughborough and hauled by a Class 5 4-6-0. No exceptional running was experienced, as was to be expected in view of the heavy traffic of a summer Saturday morning. A few passing times were as follows: MP10 17½min; St Albans (20 miles) 29min; Luton (30¼ miles) 45min; MP40 54min; Bedford (49¾ miles) 63min; Wellingborough (65 miles) 79min; MP70 84½min; Kettering (72 miles) 86min. The 52 miles from passing St Albans to the stop at Kettering therefore occupied 57 minutes. We were 1 minute late leaving Kettering, and the same at Leicester, but suffered delays costing several minutes before Derby was reached.

Interesting engines noted were Nos 41095 (15C) at Kentish Town, 92008 at Harlington, and 92009 and 51235 (an L&Y 'Pug' from Burton) at Wellingborough. A Great Eastern 'J15', No 65390, was at Kettering, and a 'J39', No 64901, was seen at Leicester, where one of the new BR Class 2 2-6-0s allocated to Kettering, No 78021, was in the shed yard. New BR '5' No 73056 was outside Derby shed.

From Derby to Crewe, on the North Stafford main line through Stoke and Kidsgrove Central, another Class 5, No 45241, was the motive power. There are nine eastbound and eight westbound trains on weekdays, stopping at most stations, but extra trains on Saturdays include through trains between Derby, Nottingham and Llandudno, calling at principal stations only.

Leaving Derby the Birmingham main line is followed through Pear Tree & Normanton and past the junction giving direct access eastwards through Trent to Nottingham. The route to Crewe then leads in a westerly direction through Tutbury (linked to Burton-on-Trent by a 5½-mile line served by auto-trains) to Uttoxeter, junction for Buxton and Macclesfield and also with the now closed GN route from Stafford, isolated from all other ex-LNER metals.

There is a small shed at Uttoxeter housing six 2-6-4Ts and a 4F 0-6-0. Turning north-west towards Stoke-on-Trent the line passes through Cresswell, junction for a short branch to Cheadle, before reaching the network of routes serving the Potteries. The station at Stoke-on-Trent has two through platforms and bays, with through tracks between the platform roads, and carriage sidings at either end. From Stoke to Crewe the route lies through Hanley and Kidsgrove Central, between which places here is an alternative loop line. At the latter a line to Macclesfield via Congleton diverges, and soon afterwards another route, to Sandbach, branches off.

There is a shed at Alsager housing 18 engines of 0-6-0, 0-6-0T and 2-6-4T types, and the important depot at Stoke-on-Trent, where 91 engines are maintained. These include 30 2-6-4Ts of Stanier, Fowler and Fairburn design, 38 4F 0-6-0s, six Stanier Class 5 4-6-0s and 14 'Jinties'. There is very little variety other than these types, and on the whole journey from Derby to Crewe, out of a great many engines recorded, the only deviations were a Class 4 2-6-0, No 43027, with an unsightly stovepipe chimney, at Tutbury, another Derby 2-6-0, No 42897, at Longport, and a 5A 2P 2-6-2T, No 41320, on a push-pull train at Kidsgrove Central. An 0-4-0ST named *Hilldale* was noted in private sidings by the lineside at Chatterley Junction, near Longport.

At Crewe a short time was spent observing the very heavy traffic before proceeding to Chester on the 4.25pm Crewe-Bangor. At Chester No 46430 (10B) was seen ex-Crewe Works. The journey to Llandudno continued on the 4.30pm ex-Liverpool (Lime Street) – 5.12pm off Chester – with through coaches to Llandudno and Afon Wen.

## SUNDAY 4 JULY 1954

During a brief spell of evening observation at Colwyn Bay a stream of return excursions was seen leaving for destinations as far afield as Henwick, Gloucestershire. Locos noted were Nos 44733 (24C), 45504 (6A), 45613, 45128 (5B), 45205, 45424 (10C), 45114, 44910, 45681 and, on the only regular train seen, 46170.

## MONDAY 5 JULY 1954

The summer 'Land Cruise' service from Llandudno began in 1951, and has operated each year since. Starting at 9.55am, the train consists of six coaches including ex-Llandudno-Manchester club cars with armchairs, open 3rds and a cafeteria car. The schedule is naturally a leisurely one, with a 2-hour stop at Barmouth and 114 continuous miles of single-track working, and the only time high speeds were attained was on the Bangor-Llandudno Junction section.

We were hauled to Rhyl by No 40095, where No 46428 backed on to act as motive power for the remainder of the journey. At Llandudno Junction the three-coach 'Welsh Dragon' express was seen, headed by No 41224. This service operates at frequent intervals between Rhyl and Llandudno, and consists of a three-coach compartment set worked as an auto-train, running non-stop between Llandudno and Colwyn Bay. At Rhyl new BR Class 7 'Pacific' No 70047, as yet unnamed, pulled in on a down express. A batch of these engines is to be stationed at Holyhead for working the 'Irish Mail' services.

Heading westwards from Rhyl, we diverged from the main line immediately in a southerly direction at Foryd Junction onto the Denbigh and Corwen branch, and were soon climbing the Clwyd valley through Rhuddlan. At Denbigh, 11 miles from Rhyl, we made a brief halt. There is a small shed here, and Nos 40072, 42566, 44073 and 52453 were seen. Just north of the station we were joined by the line from Chester via Mold, and at Ruthin we passed 2-6-2T No 41231 on a train off this route, used by about nine trains daily in each direction.

The route onwards to Corwen was closed to passenger traffic in 1953, and includes gradients as steep as 1 in 50 in a 13-mile climb to a summit 2 miles short of Corwen. We stopped here, on WR metals, to take water, and noted Nos 7431 and 52167 shunting.

The next stage, to Barmouth Junction, follows the River Dee to its source in Bala Lake, and then the line climbs at 1 in 63 to a 760-foot summit just beyond Garneddwyn Halt. Then, falling at 1 in 51 to Dolgelly, we skirted the Mawddach Estuary to Barmouth Junction, branching northwards over the swing-bridge to Barmouth station. On this stage we passed 2-6-0s Nos 6311 at Drws-y-Nant, 7310 at Dolgelly, with No 1434 on an auto-train, and No 7313 at Penmaenpool. We arrived at Barmouth at 1.55pm.

During our stay here several trains were seen, including the 2.36pm arrival from the south headed by Standard Class 2 2-6-0 Nos 78006/07, one of which came off to await the arrival of a southbound train later. Nos 4560 and 9024 were shunting empty stock. No 7800 *Torquay Manor* stood in a siding to pick up a southbound train, and a Collett '22XX' 0-6-0 was shunting in the small yard. The station has two through platforms with a bay at the north

5 July 1954: The 'Land Cruise' trains were popular with North Wales holidaymakers in the 1950s. This one, headed by Ivatt Class 2 2-6-0 No 46428, is recorded for posterity at Corwen.

end and a short bay south of the main station, from which it is separated by a level crossing.

Northwards from Barmouth the 'Cambrian' route follows the coast through Harlech, turning sharply westwards at Penrhyndeudraeth towards Pwllheli. We passed two more Collett 0-6-0s on this stretch, No 2271 at Dyffryn and 3201 at Penrhyndeudraeth, and then had a glimpse of Ffestiniog Railway sidings at Minffordd, followed by a view of the narrow-gauge railway's works at the Boston Lodge end of the causeway from Portmadoc. The latter town hosts a small Western Region loco shed, outside which were Nos 5517 and 9012/25. At Criccieth we passed No 78005, heading a passenger train, and then, at Afon Wen, where we made a brief halt, re-entered LMS territory.

Heading northward we climbed at gradients from 1 in 90 to 1 in 62 to the summit at Pant Glas, and descended at 1 in 49 to Pen-y-groes, through Dinas Junction, one-time terminus of the Welsh Highland Railway, and onwards to Caernarvon, with the Llanberis branch keeping us company through a narrow cutting on the last stage. Several of Bangor's stud of 2-6-4Ts were seen hereabouts, with 'M of S' 2-8-0 No 90187 shunting in the sidings at Caernarvon. The station here has three platforms and two bays, and marks the end of the double track, unbroken to London! After leaving Caernarvon the railway runs parallel with the Menai Straits, and a good view is obtained of the wharves at Port Dinorwic, where the slates from the Padarn quarries are shipped.

The Holyhead main line is rejoined at Menai Bridge Junction, where there are exchange sidings, and where the station has four through platforms, and shortly afterwards Bangor is reached. This is a centre of considerable importance, for local traffic starts and terminates here from the lines on Anglesey and from the Afon Wen route. The station has two island platforms, with carriage sidings and a six-road shed alongside. The allocation of 27 engines includes several Ivatt 2P and a Stanier 3P 2-6-2T, various types of 2-6-4T 4Fs, L&Y 3F and LNW 2F 0-6-0s, and a couple of Class 5s. Engines are changed here on some through trains, which in some cases make quite a lengthy stop. At the London end the main line runs immediately into a tunnel, which complicates shunting movements somewhat.

Passing through Bangor we ran along the coast through Penmaenmawr in fine style, arriving at Llandudno Junction well up to time. Here a 2P 2-6-2T took over for the short run to Llandudno, where No 44851 (5D) was noted.

## TUESDAY 6 JULY 1954

During the course of a day trip to the Isle of Man a brief visit was paid to the station at Douglas, focal point of the 3ft 0in-gauge Isle of Man Railways, which is still worked by steam throughout, and which handles a lively traffic during the brief holiday period.

From Douglas the main line runs across

6 July 1954: With one exception the locomotives of the 3ft 0in-gauge Isle of Man Railway were all 2-4-0Ts. Here, idling at Douglas, is No 12 *Hutchinson*.

towards the west coast as far as St Johns, then turns northwards along the coast through Kirk Michael and back eastward to Ramsey, thus making a great detour round the mountainous central region of the island. From St Johns a short branch continues westwards to Peel, and another, for mineral traffic, branches due south to the mines at Foxdale.

A secondary main line runs south-west from Douglas to Port Erin, keeping fairly near the coast en route.

The railway owns about 115 coaches, all compartment types and mostly bogie vehicles. There are 16 engines, all save one – an 0-6-0T for the Foxdale branch – being Beyer Peacock 2-4-0Ts of a design introduced in 1871 and somewhat enlarged through the years.

The station at Douglas has quite an imposing frontage, with two lengthy island platforms covered by umbrella roofs, and a total of six roads, plus four sidings for freight traffic. The loco depot is on one side of the main line just beyond the platforms, with two tracks plus one track in the adjoining repair shop, and there are five carriage-sidings, four covered by a shed, on the opposite side of the main line.

Although permission to inspect the shed was refused, there were several 2-4-0T engines visible in and around the station and shed: No 4 *Loch* (BP 1416/1874), No 10 *G. H. Wood* (BP4662/1905), No 12 *Hutchinson* (BP 5126/1908), No 13 *Kissach* (BP 5382/1910), No 14 *Thornhill* (BP 2028/1880, ex-MNR No 3), No 16 *Mannin* (BP 6296/1926).

### WEDNESDAY 7 JULY 1954

Leaving Llandudno on the 11.05am, connecting at the Junction with the 9.20am Crewe-Holyhead train, we travelled as far as

6 July 1954: No 10 *G. H. Wood*, a Beyer Peacock product of 1908, awaits departure from Douglas.

6 July 1954: With just a single passenger, 'one horsepower' is adequate to keep this tram moving along Douglas promenade.

Bangor on the latter. Heading westwards, soon after the Llandudno branch has diverged, the main line plunges into the Conway Tubular Bridge, and through the castle walls, inside which Conway station is situated. The railway then skirts the base of the lofty, quarry-scarred cliffs of Penmaenmawr, and a glimpse can be had of a tiny vertical-boilered engine (De Winton & Co, Caernarvon) in the quarry sidings on the seaward side of the line. Near here, also, 27 LNW carriages are stored on a long siding.

On arrival at Bangor an inspection of the shed yard showed one of Chester's BR Class 5 4-6-0s, No 73041, waiting between trips, and No 90212 from Mold Junction.

Adjacent to the harbour of Bangor proper is Port Penrhyn, where in addition to the LMR sidings are exclusive sidings and a small engine shed belonging to the Penrhyn Quarry Railway. The quarries and wharves are connected by a 1ft 11½in line opened in 1801, with a length of 6 miles, much of which is close to the Bethesda branch. Engines took over from horses in

1876, and there are about 30 all told, most of which shunt on the various levels of the quarry. There are three Hunslet 0-4-0STs for 'main line' work, the remainder being small 0-4-0STs and vertical-boilered four-wheelers, of which there are two in service.

At the wharves 'main line' engine *Blanche* (Hunslet, 1893) and cabless 0-4-0ST *Winifred* (Hunslet, 1885) were seen and photographed.

We continued to Holyhead on the 1.55pm stopping train from Bangor, engine No 45392. Soon after crossing Robert Stephenson's Britannia Tubular Bridge, opened in 1850 and linking the Isle of Anglesey to the mainland, Llanfair PG station is reached, with the full name 'Llanfairpwllgwyngyllgogerychwyrndrobwllllantysiliogogoch' displayed in the rustic woodwork on both platforms. The next station is Gaerwen, junction for the Amlwch and, at one time, the Red Wharf Bay branches. For most of the way across Anglesey the route is somewhat featureless, until after passing Valley station the line is carried on an embankment across to Holy Island, and the quays and sidings of Holyhead come into view.

The engine shed, to the right of the line, has four tracks and houses 19 engines, mostly Class

7 July 1954: Parked in a siding at Holyhead is the shed's only 4P 'Compound' 4-4-0, No 41124.

5s (nine) and rebuilt 'Royal Scots' (six), with one 'Compound' 4-4-0 and three 'Jinties'.

A visit was made to the shed and the following were noted: Nos 41124, 42976 (6D), 44864/68, 44681, 45060, 45110/80, 46147 (1B). The 'Jinties', Nos 47368/71 and 47476, were shunting on the quays and sidings.

The station consists of two platforms that fan out onto the two long jetties, with the imposing station building in between them. The BR steamers *Cambria* and *Hibernia* (5,000 tons) were moored alongside, and we made a brief inspection of the former.

We returned to Llandudno Junction on the 4.25pm stopping train, hauled of course by a Class 5. It is interesting to note that in the summer the arrival of the Irish Mail steamer at 11.55pm is followed by departures at 1.25am (to Birmingham), 1.35am (to Euston) and 1.50am (to Manchester Exchange). These are Saturdays-only, there being two trains for the corresponding weekday arrivals.

## THURSDAY 8 JULY 1954

A train leaves Llandudno each morning at 9.45am, consisting of three non-corridor coaches hauled by any available engine, as far as Llandudno Junction only, where connection is made with an excursion from Rhyl to Llanberis. The branch from Caernarvon to Llanberis is closed to all regular passenger traffic, but is served by two excursion trains every weekday during the summer months.

The train consisted of seven coaches including an observation car, hauled in both directions by 2-6-4T No 42178, stopping at all stations to Caernarvon excepting Aber. The branch is steeply graded, and after falling sharply away from the Afon Wen line climbs continuously throughout its 9-mile length, with a ruling gradient of 1 in 62. There were three intermediate stations and a halt, all now closed. A military stores depot just outside Llanberis is served by several sidings and the terminus itself has a small goods yard. The station has one long platform and a bay, in which one-coach train headed by No 42444 was ready to leave for Caernarvon at 1.00pm.

The Snowdon Mountain Railway has a gauge of 2ft 7½in, is just under 5 miles long and was opened in 1895. It is worked on the Abt rack system by seven 0-4-2T engines, all built by the Swiss Locomotive Works, Winterthur. They are numbered 2-8, No 1 having been destroyed in 1896 after being in service for only one year. Details of engines are as follows: No 2 *Enid* (SLW, 1895), No 3 *Wyddfa* (SLW, 1895), No 4 *Snowdon* (SLW, 1896), No 5 *Moel Siabod* (SLW, 1896), No 6 *Padarn* (SLW, 1922), No 7 *Aylwyn* (SLW, 1923), and No 8 *Eryri* (SLW, 1923).

The locos have inclined boilers and outside cylinders 11¼in by 23¾in, with driving wheels of 2ft 1¼in diameter. Speed is limited to 5mph and the journey time is 1 hour. Trains consist of one coach pushed up the mountain, and there are three intermediate passing-places and one halt. Llanberis is 350 feet above sea level and the summit is 3493 feet, so the *average* gradient is just less than 1 in 8! At places the line overhangs a sheer drop of many hundreds of feet, whilst elsewhere it plunges through rock cuttings, curving sharply most of the time. At the summit there is a café owned by the company.

We saw engines Nos 2/4/5/8 at Llanberis, No 2 being out of service in the small three-road shed. No 6 was our train engine, and No 3 was passed at Clogwyn and No 7 at Hebron.

At the foot of the mountain are two lakes, Llyn Padarn and Llyn Peris, which lie end-to-end connected by a small stream and behind which rise the Llanberis quarries. These are connected to the Menai Straits at Port Dinorwic by a 6-mile 4ft 0in-gauge line opened in 1824, and worked by steam engines since 1848. Narrow-gauge systems of 1ft 10¼in gauge were opened in 1870 at the quarries and quayside, and there are currently three 0-6-0Ts on the 4ft 0in gauge and about 15 assorted 0-4-0STs on the narrow gauge, most of the latter being Hunslet engines. There are additionally a few Ruston & Hornsby diesel and Planet petrol engines in use.

We soon saw 0-4-0ST *Cackler*, 0-4-0ST *Sybil* and Planet No 1 at work in the quarry, and then located the repair shops, in a series of

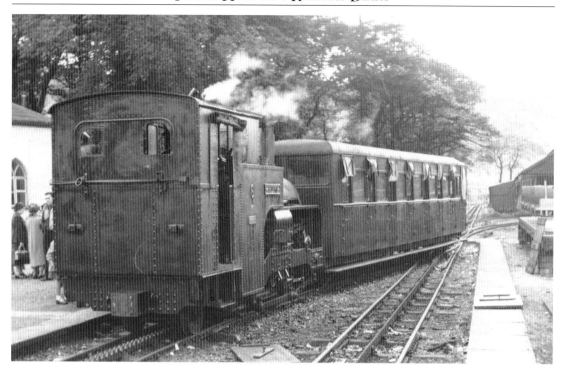

*Above* 8 July 1954: About to push its carriage to the summit is Swiss-built Snowdon Mountain Railway 0-4-2 rack tank No 6 *Padarn* at Llanberis.

*Below* 8 July 1954: The North Wales quarries were home to a fleet of 1ft 11½in-gauge 0-4-0STs. One such, at Padarn Quarry, is *Cackler* (Hunslet, 1898) with a trainload of slates.

buildings built round a courtyard in the form of a square, entered through an archway by dual-gauge tracks and linked by numerous turntables.

We were kindly escorted round the premises by a guide and found two 4-foot-gauge and three 1ft 10¾in-gauge steam engines under repair, and a Planet and Ruston engine in the 'diesel shop'. Last but not least we were shown one of the original 4ft 0in-gauge engines, *Fire Queen* of 1848, carefully preserved in an adjacent building along with a couple of primitive PW hand-trolleys. Details of engines seen are as follows:

**4ft gauge**
0-6-0T *Dinorwic* (HLC 302/1882; rebuilt after four years out of service)
0-6-0T *Velinheli* (HLC 631/1895; under repair)

**1ft 10¾in gauge**
0-4-0ST *Cackler* (HLC 671/1898)
0-4-0ST *Sybil* (Bagnall 1760/1906; cabless)
0-4-0ST *Maid Marian* (HLC 822/1902; cabless)
0-4-0ST *Jerry M* (HLC 638/1895)

0-4-0ST *Elider* (Avonside 2071/1933)
0-4-0ST petrol   No 1 (Planet 2792)
0-4-0ST petrol No 3c (Planet 2791)
0-4-0ST diesel No D1 (R & H)

**4ft gauge (preserved)**
0-4-0 tender engine *Fire Queen* (A. Horlock & Co, Northfleet, 1848)

On the return journey, between Llandudno Junction and Llandudno we were hauled by Class 5 No 44740.

## FRIDAY 9 JULY 1954

For the last trip westwards we had No 45632 *Tonga* as far as Bangor, on the 11.25am from Llandudno Junction. An interesting engine seen at the junction was 2-6-0 No 42893 (11E), which was seen returning eastwards on the following day.

The 12.35pm Bangor-Amlwch consisted of three non-corridors headed by No 41233. At

9 July 1954: With plenty of coal left in their tenders, 'Jubilee' No 45632 *Tonga* and Class 5 No 44841 leave Bangor for Holyhead.

Gaerwen No 41212 was shunting, and No 41200 came off the branch on a short goods train. The branch is single track, and undulates sharply, with a ruling gradient of 1 in 65. There are five intermediate stations, and at one of these, Llangwyllog, we passed No 41239 heading an Officers' inspection saloon. Just outside Amlwch there is a group of new sidings, one of which is extended across the road towards the waterfront. The station itself has one platform only, and a small yard in which No 41230 was shunting.

The summer timetable gives five through services in the down direction on weekdays, the first in the morning being non-stop Bangor-Gaerwen. In the opposite direction there are four through trains only, one of which conveys a through carriage to Llandudno Junction. Three of these trains do not stop between Gaerwen and Bangor. There are additionally two up trains to Gaerwen, making connections there for Bangor, and one down train adopts the same procedure. There are two extra trains on Saturdays.

We returned to Bangor by bus and saw LNW 'Cauliflower' No 58394 outside the loco shed. We returned to Llandudno on the 4.20pm stopping train. The 5.00pm to Llandudno Junction only had new 4-6-2 No 70046 at the head.

## SATURDAY 10 JULY 1954

Llandudno station on a Saturday morning presents a scene of intense activity. There are long-distance departures at 9.45am, 9.55am, 10.15am, 10.30am, 11.00am, 11.30am, 12.05pm, 12.20pm, 12.30pm, 1.05pm, 1.15pm, 1.20pm and 1.40pm, to give a 4-hour period. During this period at the height of the season there are no fewer than 20 arrivals, and in addition to this traffic there were two extra trains, comprised of non-corridor stock, to Tyldesley, Lancs – a total of 35 trains in 4 hours

to be handled over a double-track branch 3 miles long, all trains stopping at the intermediate station, and with only five platforms available.

While we waited for a period between 10.30am and 1.00pm the following were noted on arrivals: Nos 61209 (38D) with the 5.55am from Nottingham (Victoria), 45332 (10B), 45234 (26A), 45559, and 45429 (2A) with the 6.30am Leamington Spa-Llandudno.

Due to extreme delay to the second Tyldesley train, our empty stock was about 40 minutes late, and our train, the 12.20pm, due in Euston 5.25pm, was about 45 minutes late away, with engine No 45603 *Solomon Islands* and 13 coaches. After making our scheduled stops at Deganwy, Llandudno Junction, Colwyn Bay and Rhyl we were frequently and severely delayed along the coast, having hopelessly lost our path in the incessant flow of traffic. Having passed over the troughs at reduced speed we were forced to stop for water at Chester for about 10 minutes, and then made a further stop at Crewe to set down a passenger for Liverpool who had been misdirected onto the train at Deganwy! After further checks outside Stafford, a 5-minute stand at Rugby station and a prolonged halt on Camden bank, we arrived at Euston about 75 minutes late.

At Llandudno Junction a Caledonian 12-wheeled coach was seen. The Holywell Town branch train had No 41276, and a large 0-4-0ST was noted working in the oil storage sidings at Holywell Junction

Interesting observations at Chester were Nos 45368 (12A), unpainted, and 42551 (26F), both just out of Crewe Works.

At Crewe South new diesel No 13051 was at work in the yards, and at Stafford MR 1F No 41860 from Upper Bank (87K) was seen marshalled in a freight train hauled by No 48307.

Diesel No 12009 was at work at Watford, and No 45079 (25H) stood outside Euston with the empty carriage shunting engines.

# NINE ELMS AND BATTERSEA LOCO DEPOTS

*F*rom *my Wandsworth home a 20-minute bus ride and a walk through the Battersea back-streets brought me to these two vast Southern Region depots – this time with permits! Both sheds then had allocations in excess of 100, but little did I then know that, some 12 years later, I would again be at Nine Elms on that fateful 'last day of Southern steam'.*

The most interesting engine on either shed was undoubtedly the BR '5' at Nine Elms, No 73074, en route from Patricroft to Bath shed. Otherwise, Nine Elms produced the usual crop of 'Pacifics' and 4-6-0s, the latter of all classes, with one 'U' Class 2-6-0 and two 'Q1s'.

The LSWR was represented by 'D15' No 30465, 'T9s' Nos 30718/19, '700s', 'M7s' and a solitary 'O2', No 30224. Two LBSC 'E4' radial tanks completed the story.

At Battersea a good variety of types were represented among the 63 engines noted – rather a large number for a Saturday morning.

No fewer than 14 'King Arthurs' were on shed, including several in store, while 'Merchant Navy', 'Battle of Britain' and 'Britannia' 4-6-2s, 'U1' and 'N' 2-6-0s, 'Schools', 'L1' and 'E1' 4-4-0s, 'Q1' and 'C' 0-6-0s, 'W' 2-6-4Ts, 'P' and 'E2' 0-6-0Ts, an 'E4' 0-6-2T, an 'H2' 4-4-2, and LMR 2-6-4T and 2-6-2Ts make a total of 18 classes.

23 April 1955: The 'Lord Nelson' 4-6-0 was one of my favourite classes, so it was a pleasure to find one posed for a photograph at Nine Elms shed. This is No 30860 *Lord Hawke.*

*Left* 23 April 1955: A locomotive contrast at Nine Elms – one of Bulleid's masterpieces, 'Merchant Navy' No 35021 *New Zealand Line* with a veteran Drummond 'T9' 4-4-0 at the rear.

*Below left* 23 April 1955: A 'Knight of the Round Table', 'N15' 4-6-0 No 30455 *Sir Launcelot* awaits the call to duty at Nine Elms.

*Above* 23 April 1955: 'H15' 4-6-0 No 30487 of 1914 vintage at Nine Elms.

*Below* 23 April 1955: Nine Elms shed's oldest inhabitant on that day is Adams 'O2' 0-4-4T No 30224, built there in 1892.

*Above* 23 April 1955: The massive coaling tower at Battersea shed forms a backdrop to ex-SECR 'H' 0-4-4T No 31265, resting between shunting duties.

*Below* 23 April 1955: The 'Night Ferry' was one of the heaviest passenger trains on BR, hence the need for a pilot locomotive. 'L1' 4-4-0 No 31755 is being groomed for this duty at Battersea shed.

# FRIDAY 20-SUNDAY 22 MAY 1955
# SOUTH WALES TOUR

*South Wales, with its network of lines once owned by several independent companies, had been a favourite venue for my friends and myself since we had first ventured there during the war years. This time, in the course of three hectic days, we covered a multitude of new branch lines and renewed our acquaintance with many of the locomotive classes working exclusively in this area.*

### FRIDAY 20 MAY 1955

The 6.55pm ex-Paddington, calling at Reading and Newport only, contrived to lose 18-20 minutes en route, of which a slowing to 5mph over a road bridge under repair west of Swindon accounted for about 5 minutes, while the inevitable check before entering the Severn Tunnel also contributed. Between Southall and Maidenhead three of the '56XX' 0-6-2Ts stationed in the London area were seen on freight trains.

### SATURDAY 21 MAY 1955

Our systematic campaign to traverse as much as possible of the complex network of routes in South Wales met with further success during this day's intensive travels, in the course of which 17 trains were used, giving an average journey of only 4¼ miles! Since our earliest visits were planned with little thought for future problems, we find ourselves left with isolated branches or sections spread across the map from Blaenavon in the east to Brynamman in the west, and although the total remaining mileage is proportionally small, several more expeditions would be necessary to accomplish our aim.

We started off well, by disposing of two short branches, first from Cardiff (General) to Clarence Road, and then from Bute Road to Queen Street. The former, running through the

21 May 1955: Could this be the shortest passenger run on British Railways? Ex-GWR 2-6-2T No 5534 awaits departure from Cardiff (Bute Road) for Queen Street, just 1 mile away.

*Above* 21 May 1955: Much use was made of auto-trains on the South Wales branches. This one, at Senghenydd, has been propelled from Caerphilly by '4575' Class 2-6-2T No 5568.

*Below* 21 May 1955: A rare sight in South Wales, other than on the east-west main line, was a train hauled by a tender locomotive. This one, at Machen with Class 2 2-6-0 No 46520 in charge, is en route from Newport to Brecon.

least prepossessing districts in dockland, ends at a single-track terminus with a simple station building, and a run-round loop alongside the platform road. Our engine for this brief journey was 0-6-2T No 6647.

Bute Road station is much more imposing, with an island platform alongside which there are a number of carriage sidings. Our train for the 4-minute run to Queen Street was powered by 2-6-2T No 5534. Also seen in the near vicinity of the station were Nos 4161, 4632, 5698 (86J) and 6402.

At Queen Street we changed, continuing to Caerphilly on the 9.55am, engine No 4101, which tackled manfully the sharp climb up the Rhymney Railway main line through Llanishen, through the mile-long tunnel beyond Cefn On, past the carriage sheds and locomotive works and into the respectable station with its four through platforms and bay. Several standard GWR engines including a Collett 0-6-0 were seen ex-works, but much more interesting was TV 0-6-0T No 193 ('Phwllrebog' type) working in a coal-mine yard opposite the locomotive works.

The next new ground was the Senghenydd branch (opened 1894), just over 3½ miles long, which leaves the RR main line at Aber Junction halt. It is single track and, like all the valley branches, climbs steadily to a terminus hemmed in by hills. The station is quite simple, with one platform only, and enjoys quite a good service, with over a dozen daily trains each way. There are two intermediate stations. Another 2-6-2T, No 5568, with a two-coach auto-train, was working the branch. Near Abertridwr we saw an 0-4-0T named *Kitchener* and another derelict saddle-tank, in a coal-mine yard.

From Caerphilly we then travelled to Machen and back in an auto-train powered by 0-6-0PT No 6411. Between Gwernydomen Halt, a mile from Caerphilly, and White Hart Halt, just short of Machen, the up and down lines separate. The down line, the first to be laid, involved earthworks that prevented doubling the existing route save at prohibitive cost, so a new line was later laid, with one intermediate halt, and is now used for up trains

only. In this direction we were on new ground again, as last August we were too late arriving at Caerphilly to catch the connection back again!

Machen station is on the B&M route from Bassaleg Junction, Newport, to Brecon via Bargoed and Pontsticill Junction, and we saw a train on this route hauled by LMR 2MT 2-6-0 No 46520, one of a stud that has replaced the 'Dean Goods' 0-6-0s at Brecon shed.

From Caerphilly we headed northwards on the 12.40pm Rhymney train as far as Bargoed, traversing one side of the famed triangle, between Ystrad Mynach and Hengoed (scene of some 'sharp practice' with single and return tickets on 5 June 1953!). No 5670 was the engine on this stretch, with No 5605 from Bargoed to Dowlais. The latter had a two-coach train, which embarked a crowd of miners. The enginemen told us they rarely have to continue beyond Pant, where the loco has to run round the train, which it then backs northwards towards Pontsticill before running forward down to Dowlais (Central), 1½ miles.

We last traversed this B&M line, with its wild moorland scenery, on 2 June 1951, when we travelled from Newport as far as Dowlais Top. This time, at Pant, we could see snow lying thickly on the Beacons, and the day, alternately dull and bright, was made chilly by the stiff breeze. The branch has two down and one up trains on Saturdays, and terminates at a ramshackle one-track station, with an engine shed alongside. This was occupied by 0-6-0PT No 4616. There is a sharply curving connection just outside the yard limits onto the LNWR Abergavenny-Merthyr line.

After a brisk walk and bus ride to Merthyr, we caught the 3.00pm Cardiff train as far as Llandaff headed by No 5661 (88D). Though interesting, this TVR route is all 'old ground', through Pontypridd and Abercynon. We saw plenty of traffic, as always in the vicinity of Pontypridd, but most interesting was the glimpse of LNWR 0-6-2 'Coal Tanks' Nos 58891 and 58926, from Abergavenny, stored outside Abercynon shed.

We walked across from Llandaff to Coryton Halt, terminus of a short double-track branch

*Above* 21 May 1955: This is Dowlais Central, with 0-6-2T No 5605 running round its train after arrival from Bargoed.

*Left* 21 May 1955: 'Auto 3', headed by 0-6-0T No 6416, has arrived at Coryton Halt with a service from Cardiff (Queen Street).

off the Rhymney Railway main line from just south of Heath Halt, which has platforms on both the main and the branch. The latter originally continued to serve the Nantgarw Colliery and the Treforest area, but now stops just beyond the road bridge north of Coryton. We travelled down to Queen Street in the auto-train, with engine No 6416.

Our next journey followed almost immediately, from Cardiff General to Pontypridd, the interesting point being that the route followed was along the main line to St Fagans, thence round the spur onto the Barry Railway route, which extends southwards through Wenvoe to Cadoxton. This line climbs high to the west of the valley of the Taff, then descends to join the TVR main line at Treforest. Once again we had a '64XX' engine,

No 6438. Onwards from Pontypridd to Porth we travelled in an extra train hauled by 0-6-2T No 5677 and after the arrival of the regular train behind BR Class 3 2-6-2T No 82000 of Barry shed, we boarded the well-filled auto-train powered by 2-6-2T No 5572. The Maerdy branch penetrates a somewhat barren valley with many evidences of derelict mines, and the principal place served is Ferndale, one station short of the terminus, where there is a substantial two-road shed, and a couple of 0-6-2Ts were noted here. At Maerdy there is the customary single-track station with loop alongside, and a number of sidings that extend past the station to the head of the valley. A small shed housed another two-car train, which, with engine No 5572, took over the service. There were no signs of habitation in the immediate vicinity of the station, and a lonely road with an infrequent bus service climbs up the hillside in the direction of Aberdare. The branch is double track.

Back at Porth our train to Cardiff arrived behind No 82000, the only BR Standard tank we saw all day despite the extensive stud now stationed at Barry. On the way, passing Radyr and Cathays, we saw plenty of traffic, and engines Nos 6651 (86J) at Radyr and 8448 (86F) at Cardiff General were noteworthy – and so the day's voyaging came to an end.

## SUNDAY 22 MAY 1955

The only travelling other than the journey home was to Barry Island and back via Penarth. The island is linked to the mainland by a causeway carrying the road and railway and the station, though having only one platform, is substantially built, with carriage sidings adjacent. At Barry itself the main buildings have been rebuilt, but the disreputable awnings on the island platform remain.

At the shed 63 engines were recorded, including eight of the BR Standard 3MT 2-6-2Ts. The majority were 0-6-2Ts ('56XX' and TV

classes) and 0-6-0Ts ('16XX', '37XX', '84XX', '64XX') with one or two of the larger 2-8-2 mineral tanks and a couple of 2-6-2Ts of Classes '55XX' and '41XX'.

At the station, LNWR 0-8-0 No 49409 arrived with an excursion from the Tredegar area.

A quick tour of Canton shed produced the usual variety of tender engines including 'Castles', 'Halls', 'Granges', BR Class 7 4-6-2s, Class 5 and 4 4-6-0s, 'M of S' and '28XX' 2-8-0s, '43XX' 2-6-0s, and tank engines of 2-8-2, 2-8-0, 0-6-2 and 0-6-0 wheel arrangements. The only non-standard engine was Alexandra Docks Railway 2-6-2T No 1205, inside the roundhouse.

After travelling as far as Newport on the 1.05pm Bristol stopping train and indulging in some complicated reversals at Marshfield, we visited Ebbw Junction shed.

Here, among over 140 engines recorded, the principal feature was the batch of 2-10-0s, Nos 92000-06, which are used on heavy freight traffic to and from Ebbw Vale. There were also,

22 May 1955: Nicely posed for the camera at Barry shed is '5100' 2-6-2T No 4177.

*Above*  22 May 1955: Ex-Taff Vale Railway Class 'A' 0-6-2T No 308, also seen at Barry shed, was outshopped by Vulcan Foundry in 1921 and later substantially rebuilt by the GWR.

*Below*  22 May 1955: This '7200' 2-8-2T, No 7252, was also photographed at Barry shed; it was originally a 2-8-0T, but had its bunker lengthened to enable it to work further afield than the South Wales valleys.

22 May 1955: 'Castle' 4-6-0 No 5054 *Earl of Ducie* is 'Not to be Moved' as it stands over the ash-pit at Cardiff Canton shed.

of course, plenty of GWR and 'M of S' 2-8-0s, among them old No 2800, now in its 53rd year. Now the 'Deans' have vanished from the scene the only 0-6-0s were several '2251' Class. The inevitable serried ranks of 2-8-2Ts and 2-8-0Ts looked little different from our last and only previous visit on 12 June 1949. Among the host of 'panniers', however, all the 'unstandards' had gone, and two new '16XX' Class, Nos 1653/56, helped fill the vacancy. Two '61XX' 2-6-2Ts, Nos 6102/14, and veteran Nos 3170 and 3103 provided some variety, and the repair shops were occupied by Nos 4264 (86J), 4593 (86H), 7736, 8710 and 5074. BR 4-6-0 No 75021 (86C) was in the yard.

The 5.05pm to London, non-stop, gave us a fairly good run, recovering from an 8-minute-late start and some severe checks en route, albeit with an easy 3-hour schedule. Engine No 5054 *Earl of Ducie* was responsible, with some sustained running around the 65mph mark for considerable distances. Outside Swindon Works new 0-6-0T No 1669 contrasted with Nos 205/11, 683 and 2183 'heading for the last round-up'.

Also noted were Nos 41310, 7811 and, heartening sight, 'Star' No 4061 *Glastonbury Abbey* ex-works and resplendent in full passenger livery.

The last item of interest was brand-new 2-6-0 No 76054 of Redhill, seen in Reading (SR) station.

# Saturday 6 August 1955
# North and East London

*A*n advantage of living in London was having easy access to four of the six BR Regions, even if the journey across the City by bus and Underground could be tedious. On this and the next outing a good variety of steam traction was encountered, from redundant 'Tilbury' tanks to newly built 2-10-0s, not to mention – an ominous sign of things to come – a few diesel shunters!

*A* run out to Wood Green and back and a spell of observation produced nothing noteworthy, though there was plenty of passenger traffic, with numerous filthy 'V2s' taking a hand, as is invariably the case at holiday times.

At Barking traffic was brisk and a good selection of BR tanks were seen in a fairly short period, although plenty of LMR 2-6-4Ts and a couple of 3P 4-4-2Ts, Nos 41969/77, were at work, the latter on lightly loaded Tilbury trains. The new aluminium District Line train was seen, unpainted save for a thin red line at waist height.

Evidence of the possible demise of the LTS 0-6-2Ts in the near future was offered by the sight of one of these engines in Bow Works yard and another in Plaistow shed yard, both in woebegone condition.

6 August 1955: Condenser-fitted 3P 2-6-2T No 40040 runs round its train at Barking after arrival from St Pancras.

# LONDON AREA

A fairly comprehensive tour began with a run up from Clapham Junction to Waterloo, when 'D15' No 30465 was seen on an arrival at about 10.45am. Thence from Euston to Willesden, where Old Oak and Willesden shed yards were viewed from the canal bank, without anything of great interest being seen. En route from Euston there was plenty of traffic to watch, and Newton Heath 'Jubilee' No 45700 *Amethyst* was one of the many engines seen.

From Willesden a leisurely journey to Broad Street was made, several freight trains being passed, one of which was hauled by an SR 'Q1' 0-6-0. At the North London terminus ample evidence was afforded of its function as a relief to King's Cross by the presence of two 'N2s' and two 'B1s'.

At Liverpool Street there was all the hustle to be expected on a busy summer Saturday morning. At that particular time all the engines happened to be of the customary classes – 'Britannia' 4-6-2s and 'B1', 'B12/3' and 'B17' 4-6-0s – but during a fairly lengthy spell of observation at Stratford the variety was a little better, with Stratford's '76000' 2-6-0s in force on Clacton and Walton area up trains, supplemented by LMR 4F 2-6-0 No 43093 of South Lynn, ex-Stratford Works, and 'J39' No 64782 running tender-first on a train from Walton-on-Naze. At Bishopsgate two of the new diesels, Nos 11121/22, were outside the little shed with one 'J69' tank.

In the course of the journey through Temple Mills yard a great many engines were recorded, with three 2-10-0s in line at the far end (Nos 92012/43 of March, and one other). 'J17' No 65511 stood on a siding near the Stratford end with the centre pair of driving wheels removed,

20 August 1955: Almost 40 years after entering service, an ex-LNWR 'Oerlikon' electric unit rests quietly at Broad Street station.

*Above* 20 August 1955: The 'B17' 'Sandringham' 4-6-0s were designed with the Great Eastern section in mind, so No 61634 *Hinchingbrook* passing Stratford is very much on its home ground.

*Left* 20 August 1955: With motive power at a premium on this Saturday, humble Class 4 2-6-0 No 76034 heads a Clacton to Liverpool Street express through Stratford.

and when passing the 'Field' a Great Central 4-4-2T, unidentified, could be seen.

From the rolling stock point of view the usual collection of antiques had been pressed into service on the main-line trains. By contrast, the quintuple articulated sets on the North Woolwich-Palace Gates branch have been freshly painted and look quite dazzling.

Near Copper Mill Junction the solitary 'K5', No 61853, was noted on an up passenger train.

On the Great Northern, Hornsey shed yard displayed two more 9F 2-10-0s and several quite clean 'M of S' 2-8-0s. An interesting engine on the main line, running light, was 'K3' No 61974 (38A). The New England 'B1s' were out in force, and the 4.00pm down Cleethorpes had No 61082 (40B). 'W1' No 60700 went down soon after with an express, while the up 'Yorkshire Pullman' had a filthy 'V2'.

# Sunday 10-Wednesday 13 June 1956
# North East England tour

*T*he four days covered by these notes were part of a ten-day 'marathon' commencing in Lincolnshire and concluding in Cumbria and Lancashire. The 'North Eastern' part of the tour began in York and encompassed the highly industrial areas of the Tyne and Tees, with much heavy freight traffic, contrasting with single-track lines in unspoiled countryside. The whole trip covered more than 1,500 miles of rail travel and added more than 160 locomotives – nearly all of them steam – to my 'score'.

### Sunday 10 June 1956

The day's travelling, being Sunday, was the lowest of the tour, as the services from York to the coast in the winter timetable consist of a group of morning and evening trains, with a long gap in between. We left York on the 10.17am, a Leeds to Scarborough train hauled by 'D49' No 62749 *The Cottesmore*.

Access to the Scarborough and Hull routes out of York is gained by branching very sharply to the right at the north end of the station,

across the main line to Newcastle, and after threading a residential district of the city the two routes diverge at Bootham Junction almost 2 miles out. All the intermediate stations between York and Malton, and Malton and Seamer (on the outskirts of Scarborough and junction for the coastal route southwards through Bridlington) are closed, and the standard journey time is almost 50 minutes non-stop, or an hour with the two stops, for the 42 miles. The country traversed in flat until the neighbourhood of Seamer, where the line

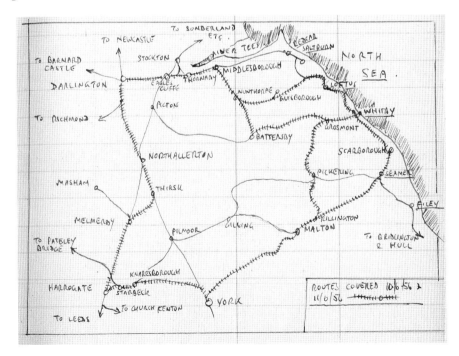

*Above* 10 June 1956: No 67289 of 1899 vintage was one of three ex-NER 'G5' 0-4-4Ts stabled at Malton shed. It was fated for withdrawal at the end of the year.

*Below* 10 June 1956: With 'express' headlights in position, Class 'D49/2' 'Hunt' 4-4-0 No 62749 *The Cottesmore* is ready to leave Scarborough shed.

climbs for several miles at about 1 in 200 to Scarborough. Running is quite brisk, and loads generally are around the eight-to-ten-coach mark.

Malton station has two platforms, one being an island separated from the main down platform by only one track. Access to the island is via a movable bridge when no train occupies the down line. There is a two-road shed with an allocation of about a dozen engines – mostly 0-6-0s with a few 'G5s' and a 4-6-2T – at the western end of the station. Two lines link with the York-Scarborough route, one from Driffield and one from Pilmoor on the Newcastle main line, but there are no passenger services on either. At Rillington, about 3 miles before Scarborough, the line from Whitby and Pickering is joined.

Scarborough has two stations, both termini. One, Londesborough Road, is used for certain summer weekend trains and excursions only, and is alongside the lines leading into Central station. The latter has a pleasing and imposing building, but the platform arrangement is unusual, the six or so platforms being staggered. Two extend alongside the buildings, the others terminate at varying distances short of these two. There are some carriage sidings alongside the station and others out as far as the shed, which is about a mile from the station.

**Scarborough (50E):** The shed consists of two buildings facing each other, but the one nearest the station, formerly a roundhouse, is now used as an Engineer's Department workshop. The other, a short eight-road building, is ample for the allocation of 14 engines – 'D49s', 'A8s', LMR 2-6-4Ts and a solitary 'J72'. The yard is quite spacious and on a busy day would be needed to deal with the motive power arriving on excursion trains.

The list of engines on shed is: 'B16' Nos 61427/45, 'B1' No 61255, 'V2' No 60864, 'D49' Nos 62726/35/39/56/69/70, 'A8' Nos 69881/85, LMR 2-6-4T Nos 42084/85, 'J72' No 69016 and 'J25' No 65687, a total of 16.

At 6.00pm we left for Whitby, in a Middlesbrough train hauled by 'L1' No 67754.

The Whitby line makes a trailing junction just beyond the platform ends, so our engine was against the buffers, and backed us out beyond the junction. Threading a residential quarter and passing under several road bridges, we passed a fairly extensive goods yard, and some more carriage sidings, and were soon climbing steadily. For 21 miles to Whitby the line is always near the cliffs, passing such well-known scenic spots as Robin Hood's Bay and Ravenscar. There are no Sunday trains in the winter months, but four run southbound in the morning and northbound in the evening commencing on 20 May, one to Darlington, one to West Hartlepool, one to Stockton and one to Middlesbrough. Only one train calls at practically all stations, the rest being 'semi-fast', though high speeds are out of the question thanks to steep grades and sharp reverse curves. On winter weekdays there are only three trains daily each way between Whitby and Scarborough, and between Whitby and Middlesbrough.

**Whitby (50G):** This shed was visited in the evening, a two-road building on the river bank, not far from Town station. The allocation is about 12 strong, now consisting of three BR 3MT 2-6-0s, five BR 2-6-4Ts, a couple of 'A8' 4-6-2Ts and two 'J25' 0-6-0s. Engines on shed were: BR 2-6-0 Nos 77013/4, 2-6-4T Nos 80116/7/8/9/20, 'A8' No 69876, LMR 2-6-4T No 42083 and 'J25' No 45663 (with snowplough fitted).

## MONDAY 11 JUNE 1956

This was one of the heaviest day's programmes of the tour, covering all routes remaining open in the Malton-Whitby-Middlesbrough area (save Saltburn, postponed until the following day), and taking us as far as Harrogate. Like the previous evenings, our travels in the coastal area were marred by mist and poor visibility, yet in the York-Harrogate-Darlington area fine weather prevailed.

The first journey was from Whitby (Town) to Malton, over the steeply graded Whitby and Pickering route. The Town station has three platforms, close to the harbour, and the small group of carriage sidings near the shed are built on a wooden pier on the river bank. The line heads inland, closely following the river, for some miles, passing under the Scarborough-Middlesbrough route, which is carried on a high viaduct. A steeply graded spur connects the two routes.

We travelled on the 9.20am ex-Whitby, 'A8' No 69877 with four non-corridor bogies. At Grosmont we branched off the inland route to Middlesbrough via Battersby (the station has platforms curving away round both routes) and then began the climb up to Goathland Moor and Pickering Moor with grades as steep as 1 in 40, through rolling country, thickly wooded in the valleys, with tumbling streams. Another 'A8', No 69890, was passed at Grosmont, running light, and 'J27' 0-6-0 No 65844 near Levisham, on a down freight.

The summit passed, we ran easily down to Pickering, where routes from Seamer (closed June 1950) and Gilling (closed February 1953) join. 'G5' No 67319, sub-shedded from Malton, was shunting. We ran very smartly over the Pickering-Malton section, 15 minutes being allowed for the 11 miles non-stop, the Scarborough route being joined at Rillington. There were five trains each way in the 1955/6 winter timetable, with two extra journeys as far as Goathland. This line, in common with most others in the area, is scheduled for early 'dieselisation'.

At Malton several 'G5' 0-4-4Ts were on shed or shunting, and although many engines of this class have already gone and the rest are scheduled for an early demise, they are still a familiar part of the NER scene. The 'A8' 4-6-2Ts, 45 strong and as yet intact, are also very much in evidence in this area. Until quite recently they practically monopolised the local passenger work, and are still strongly represented at Saltburn, Middlesbrough, etc. Built in 1913/14 as 4-4-4Ts, they were rebuilt in their present form during 1931-36.

Whilst waiting at Malton the Bradford-Scarborough through train stopped there, ten LMS corridors hauled by No 44836 (20A). We left on the 10.54am to York, a fairly long train

of non-corridor stock behind 'B1' No 61016 *Inyala*.

Traffic was brisk during an hour at York, but nothing of special interest was seen before we left for Harrogate on the 12.20pm, four coaches behind No 62758 *The Cattistock* (50D). A great number of engines of many types were recorded passing York sheds and the yards to the north of the station, before we branched off to the westwards about 2 miles out. Most of our passengers disembarked at Poppleton, the first stop, after which we did very little trade until reaching Knaresborough, the most important town en route. Seven down and six up trains use this route, with no Sunday trains (winter 1955/6), the journey time for the 20½ miles varying from 34 to 55 minutes depending on intermediate stops. Starbeck 'D49s', and an occasional 'D20', are used. The next station after Knaresborough is Starbeck, whence one arm of a triangle leads to Harrogate and the other to Ripon. Passing a medium-sized goods yard we arrived at Harrogate station, which has two through platforms and a centre through road, five passenger and a parcels bay. Lines radiate to Ripon and Northallerton, Pateley Bridge (closed), Leeds (now dieselised), Church Fenton and York.

We left on the 2.20pm to Northallerton, with 'B1' No 61216 and a train including brand-new BR corridor coaches. This train runs non-stop to Ripon (11½) miles, thence to Topcliffe, and all stations to Northallerton, and we made a speedy exit from Harrogate on an obviously favourably graded section. At Melmerby one route continues northwards to join the main line at Northallerton, and this is used by a good deal of freight traffic, but we used the line that handles practically all passenger trains, north-eastwards to Thirsk. Another line branches off at Melmerby, the Masham branch, closed to passenger traffic.

At Northallerton we had a wait of about 40 minutes due to the late running of the 3.02pm York-Newcastle express, with through carriages from Cardiff. In this time a good deal of freight traffic was seen, the mineral trains monopolised by 'M of S' 2-8-0s from a variety

*Above* 11 June 1956: During a short stay at Northallerton there was a constant procession of freights on the main line. This one is hauled by ex-NER 'B16' 4-6-0 No 61443.

*Below* 11 June 1956: Class 'J77' 0-6-0T No 68423, seen shunting at Darlington, was built in 1878 as a 'BTP' 0-4-4T. As transformed in 1904 it performed its humble but useful duties for another 53 years.

*Above* 11 June 1956: Class 'A8' 4-6-2T No 69866 heads a Saltburn train at Darlington (Bank Top). Originally a 4-4-4T, it was rebuilt in 1934.

*Below* 11 June 1956: All is quiet at Battersby, but it was once an important junction on the Grosmont to Picton line, with branches to Nunthorpe and Weardale.

of Tyneside and Teesside sheds, the fitted freights worked by 'B1', 'B16' and 'A2' Classes. Two of the Northallerton's Class 2 2-6-0s, Nos 78012/13, were seen.

On arrival at Darlington we transferred to the 4.30pm Saltburn train, headed by 'A8' No 69866. 'G5' No 67305 left on the 4.15pm to Richmond.

The Teesside traffic from Darlington is very heavy. There are passenger trains at a half-hourly average to and from Saltburn, greatly augmented to Redcar and Saltburn at holiday times, and of course an immense freight traffic is handled in the Thornaby-Middlesbrough area. The first important station is Eaglescliffe, with two island platforms, junction of lines from Darlington, Northallerton, the coast route through Stockton and West Hartlepool, and the south Teesside route through Middlesbrough. The next station is Thornaby, junction for Stockton (forming a triangle), after which the great Newport marshalling yard and locomotive depot flanks the main line on the left. To the right a site has been cleared for the new Thornaby shed to replace Newport and Middlesbrough.

Numerous diesels were at work shunting in the yards, and an endless stream of freight trains was seen, worked by 'M of S' 2-8-0s, 'Q6' 0-8-0s, 'K1' 2-6-0s and 'J26' and 'J27' 0-6-0s.

Middlesbrough station has an island platform on the down side and a single-faced platform for up trains, and is in the process of rebuilding. We changed here, and left at 6.05pm behind 'A8' No 69842 in a well-patronised train for Whitby via Battersby. This route branches from the Redcar and Saltburn line shortly after passing Middlesbrough locomotive depot and heads roughly southeast through Ormesby to Nunthorpe. Here the two routes to Whitby divide, that via Staithes forking off eastwards towards the coast, while out own continues southwards to Battersby. Here reversal is necessary, for the line turns westwards and joins the east-west line from Grosmont to Picton on the Northallerton-Eaglescliffe route.

Battersby station consists of two platforms and a bay, and after we had waited there for some minutes and our engine had run round the train, a Whitby-Middlesbrough train headed by No 69891 pulled in alongside us. The Battersby-Picton section is closed to passenger traffic. From Battersby we were in the dale of the River Esk and its tributaries, with high, rolling hills on either side. After stopping at seven intermediate stations we reached Grosmont, junction with the line from Malton, and were now retracing our steps over the route along which we had left Whitby in the morning.

The winter service provides three trains each way between Middlesbrough and Whitby, with a fourth from Battersby to Whitby and back. Journey time for the 35 miles is between 80 and 90 minutes. The scene at Whitby Town shed as we passed had more of a 'North Eastern' flavour than the previous day, as 'A8' Nos 69864/65/90 and 'J25' No 65663 were outside.

At 8.05pm we left Whitby (Town) in a one-coach train hauled by No 80120 on the shuttle service to West Cliff station. This was enveloped in mist still, which persisted, so we found, right along the coast.

Our travels continued on the 8.19pm from West Cliff (7.10pm off Scarborough), a through train to Darlington headed by 'B1' No 61255 with four coaches. As far as Middlesbrough we made only one intermediate stop, at Loftus, and although running along the coast does not allow high speeds, we certainly made lively progress once we had reached this flat country in the neighbourhood of Guisborough. The 13¼ miles from Whitby to Loftus are allowed 37 minutes, and the 21¼ miles thence to Middlesbrough 42 minutes. The coastal section involves crossing high viaducts where streams penetrate inland through deep ravines, particularly at Staithes, and beyond Loftus a great semi-circle is described, the direction changing from due north to due south within a mile or so. Here we ran out of a deeply wooded valley past a large industrial plant, which is obviously being extended, with numerous sidings in the vicinity – the first evidence of the type of scenery that predominates on Teesside. Double track begins here, and a triangle

11 June 1956: The 120 0-8-0s of Class 'Q6' were the mainstay of heavy freight haulage in North East England for more than 40 years. No 63389 is seen plodding through Middlesbrough.

junction is made with the route that follows the coast to the outskirts of Saltburn, where the Saltburn to Darlington route is joined. This is used by freight trains to and from the steelworks we had passed, and we saw such a train, headed by an 0-8-0.

We now were heading westwards, through Hutton Gate, junction for a short branch to Guisborough, to Nunthorpe, where we were joined by the line from Whitby via Battersby, and so to Middlesbrough. Despite gathering dusk, many more engines were seen in the Middlesbrough-Eaglescliffe section, and we ran into Darlington punctually at 10.14pm.

## TUESDAY 12 JUNE 1956

We left Darlington in pouring rain on the 9.00am to Saltburn, headed by 'L1' 2-6-4T No 67750. As far as Middlesbrough we were in territory covered the previous day, and once again intensive freight was noted in the

Thornaby-Middlesbrough district. Some of the largest steelworks, however, lie between Middlesbrough and Redcar, and a great many 'private owner' tank engines were seen at work.

Redcar, a holiday resort, is served by two stations, Redcar Central and Redcar East. The former has one long through platform and bay with through tracks alongside. Thereafter, industry is left behind, though the 'scenery' thence to Saltburn is drab in the extreme, with flat sandbanks on the shore and flat open country inland. Saltburn has a fairy large station with two island platforms with roofs completely devoid of glass. A two-road shed outside has an allocation of about ten 'A8s' and one LMR Class 4 2-6-0. One or two of the former and the latter, No 43054, were seen.

The same 'L1' took us back to Middlesbrough, where we changed onto the 11.35am Newcastle train, comprised of four two-car diesel sets, which we used as far as Sunderland. This involved retracing our route back towards Darlington as far as Thornaby and then using the eastern side of the triangle junction round into Stockton. We were now on an important main line used particularly in summer by through trains between King's

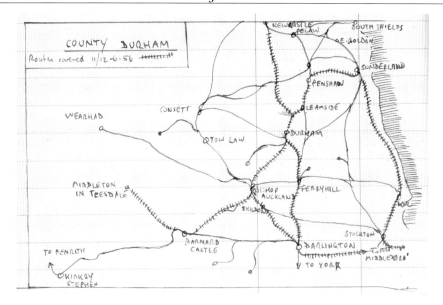

Cross, Sunderland, South Shields and Newcastle. With Stockton and the Hartlepools having populations of over 70,000 each, and Sunderland 180,000, and bearing in mind the importance of Sunderland and West Hartlepool as ports, it is easily understood that both passenger and freight traffic is heavy. There are locomotive depots at Stockton (51E, allocation 45), West Hartlepool (51C, allocation 65) and Sunderland (54A, allocation 50). Only Stockton, with about ten 'B1s', is normally concerned with express passenger traffic, but both West Hartlepool and Sunderland have a number of 'G5s' – steadily diminishing of course – for local work, with several 'A8s' also at Sunderland. The introduction of diesel railcars is changing this picture, while a number of diesel shunters of the smaller 0-6-0 and 0-4-0 types are stationed at West Hartlepool.

After leaving Stockton we were booked to call at Billingham, West Hartlepool, Seaham and Sunderland, and made some very fast running at times, particularly after a signal stop of several minutes' duration near Horden.

Stockton station has two through platforms and bays, with a centre through track, under a double-span arched roof. At West Hartlepool two of the 0-6-0 diesels, Nos 11149/51, were noted at work in the yards, where very large dumps of timber were stored.

At Sunderland we caught the 2.08pm to Durham, with 'G5' No 67342 hauling three coaches. Other 'G5s', Nos 67318/43, were at work in the vicinity of the station. The 15-mile route to Durham branches sharply away from the main line immediately south of Sunderland station, and climbs steeply onto fairly high ground on the south bank of the River Wear, which it follows fairly closely as far as Penshaw. Here it joins a north-south route, from Pelaw on the Newcastle-Sunderland line to a point a couple of miles north of Ferryhill on the Anglo-Scottish main line. It follows this route southwards as far as Leamside (station closed, consisting of a large island platform with bays) and then forks westwards to join the main line a mile north of Durham.

There are about ten trains daily each way between Sunderland and Durham, with extras on Saturdays. A number of trains commence or terminate at Bishop Auckland or Middleton-in-Teesdale. 'G5s' from Sunderland or the sub-shed at Durham are responsible. A considerable freight traffic is dealt with in this area, which is a coal-mining district. An 'M of S' 2-8-0 passed us at Hylton, and then at Cox Green an NCB 0-6-0T of obvious NER origins passed us, working a coal train along the main line. Penshaw, junction with the north-south line, has yards where 0-8-0 Nos 63342 and

63468, 0-6-0 No 65798, and NCB (No 2 area) 0-6-2T No 57 – painted bright green – were at work.

After a wait of 26 minutes at Durham we left on the 3.12pm for Barnard Castle, the same set of coaches now being hauled by 'G5' No 67258. During our wait an 'A2'-hauled northbound express received rear-end assistance from this 'G5', which halted on the viaduct south of the station and then backed into the bay at the south end, into which its train had been propelled.

The Durham-Barnard Castle route leaves the main line sharply after crossing the viaduct south of the station, and just after the triangle connecting with the Consett line and the branch to Waterhouses have diverged. There is nothing specially noteworthy about this line until Bishop Auckland is reached, and the whole of this day's journeys were made in dismal, wet weather, which spoiled the scenic attractions where they existed, as in the Middleton-in-Teesdale area.

The winter 1955-56 timetable shows eight trains each way on weekdays only (two extra on Saturdays), of which only two each way are extended as far as Barnard Castle or Middleton-in-Teesdale. The distance from Durham to Barnard Castle is 26 miles, and the one all-stations train takes 93 minutes including a 29-minute wait at Bishop Auckland.

Bishop Auckland is an important town, with routes converging from six directions. Passenger services still operate to and from Barnard Castle, Darlington, Durham and Tow Law (though the latter is scheduled for closure), and the station presents an animated scene when trains connect. The through platforms on the Durham-Darlington line are quite lengthy, and one more platform curves sharply away from these towards Tow Law. A spur without platforms completes a triangle, the main station buildings being inside the triangle.

When we arrived 'Y3' Sentinel No 68149 was shunting, and during our long wait a Crook-Darlington train stopped, headed by a '77XXX' BR 2-6-0. Our train, filled to capacity

with schoolchildren, left punctually at 4.12pm, and began the climb to the summit at Cockfield Fell. West Auckland shed, passed just before the station of that name is reached, has a substantial allocation of LMR and BR Class 2 and 3 2-6-0s as well as ex-NER 0-6-0s and tank engines, and we saw Nos 43101 and 46470/80 outside. After a smart run downhill to Barnard Castle, where a BR Class 3 2-6-2T came through on the 4.15pm Darlington-Penrith train, we changed into the three-coach Middleton branch train headed by No 77002.

The Middleton branch, single track, is 8 miles long, leaving the Penrith line about three-quarters of a mile beyond Barnard Castle and then following it closely for a short distance. There are three intermediate stations, all very small, and the terminus has a simple platform and loop, a small goods yard, and sidings serving a stone-crushing plant. There are six trains daily. This is a very picturesque line, climbing as it does up to the edge of Middleton Common overlooking the Tees Valley.

After only 10 minutes we were off back to Bishop Auckland. Approaching Barnard Castle we were held waiting for the 5.30pm Darlington-Middleton, headed by a 'G5' running bunker-first. A quick change was made here into a train hauled by an Ivatt Class 2 'Mogul'.

Although our 2-6-0 was running tender-first, we made some very fast running down from Cockfield Fell to Bishop Auckland, 27 minutes being allowed for the 15 miles non-stop. This time Nos 43055, 76048 (52C), 65731 and 68692 were seen around West Auckland shed, and during our 27-minute wait at Bishop Auckland 'A8' Nos 69856/74, 'A5' No 69841 and 'L1' No 67716 were recorded, with 'K1' No 62057 passing through on a freight.

Our engine to Darlington was No 46471. Another of this class, No 46467, was at Shildon, where Nos 68391, 68691 and 63442 were shunting. Shildon, an important centre on the Stockton & Darlington Railway, is junction for the mineral line to Stockton.

We joined the Penrith route at North Road and came slowly into Darlington on time at 7.41pm. Our connection to Newcastle, the

3.20pm ex-King's Cross, due off Darlington at 7.42pm, was waiting, heading by an 'A3', which made a fast run, non-stop, the allowance being 43 minutes for the 36½ miles. We then caught an electric train out to Jesmond where we spent the night.

## WEDNESDAY 13 JUNE 1956

The last day's travels in the NE Region began with a tour of the coastal branches north of Newcastle serving the Newbiggin/Blyth colliery area.

Journeying from West Jesmond to Monkseaton on a coast route electric train, we then changed onto the 9.22am Monkseaton-South Blyth, No 67281 with three very ancient NER non-corridors. The first 5½ miles, to Newsham, pass through Seaton Delaval and Hartley, and the famous collieries of those names contribute a heavy mineral traffic. At Seaton a branch joins from Backworth, forming an alternative route from Newcastle used by one train only on weekdays and five on Saturdays, these latter being through from Manors to Newbiggin.

At Newsham the Blyth and Newbiggin routes divide. The 1½-mile route to the former is served by a frequent shuttle service connecting with trains to and from Newbiggin, as well as the through trains between Monkseaton and Blyth. The terminus at Blyth has an island platform, and the continuation to the coal staithes runs alongside at a higher level. South Blyth shed, near the station, is still wholly 'NER' with about a dozen 0-6-0s and ten 0-4-4 and 0-6-0 tanks.

Noted in the vicinity were 0-6-0 Nos 65727/81 and 65808/62, 'G5s' Nos 67277 and 67339/41 and 'J77' No 68405.

No 67281 hauled us back to Newsham, where up trains must run through the station and back into the only platform on the Blyth line, which serves the down track. Another 'G5', No 67339, hauled us from Newsham to Newbiggin, between which several more 0-6-0s were at work, and numerous coal mines were passed. Ashington station forms a single-track bottleneck in a route that is double with this exception for some distance further. From Bedlington there is a 'goods only' branch

13 June 1956: Built in 1889 and still going strong at Hexham is 'J21' 0-6-0 No 65033.

13 June 1956: Alston, terminus of the branch from Haltwhistle, would make a good subject for modellers, with its compact layout including a small engine shed. Heading our train up and down the branch is BR Class 4 2-6-0 No 76024.

inland to Morpeth. Newbiggin station consists of a single platform with loop.

NCC engines were seen at Ashington (0-6-0ST Nos 26/42/11 and 71515) and Newbiggin (No 18). Of these, Nos 26 and 71515 were 'M of S' types (the latter is the ex-WD number) and No 11 was of much older design. These engines apparently belong to Northern Division No 3 area of the NCB.

To return to Newcastle we changed at Newsham, and again at Monkseaton onto an electric train, where parcels car No 86000 was seen.

We were soon away again on the 12.45pm stopping train to Hexham via North Wylam, engine No 76047. The 'new ground' was from Scotswood to Prudhoe, on a loop that sees only four trains daily. After leaving the main line it climbs quite steeply, and Blaydon shed can be seen across the river.

Hexham, a market town of 9,700 people, is junction for the long branch north-west through Reedsmouth to Riccarton Junction, and also for the Allendale branch, closed to passenger traffic. The small shed, sub to Blaydon, has about half-a-dozen engines

allocated, of which until recently all bar one 0-6-0 were 'G5s'. 'J21s' 65033 and 65103 and a 'V1' 2-6-2T were the only occupants.

We left at 4.54pm behind 'B1' No 61100 (52A) as far as Haltwhistle, an island platform on the bank of the river and junction for the 13-mile-long Alston branch. This terminates at the highest market town in England, and the branch climbs steeply through delightful countryside to a height of about 900 feet. The train consisted of two coaches hauled by No 76024 (52C). There are four intermediate stations, and four weekday trains, augmented on Saturdays. The station is a substantial stone building with a wooden roof spanning the simple platform and two tracks. A one-road engine shed is alongside, and there is a moderate-sized goods yard, which appeared to be dealing with a fair amount of traffic.

There are three viaducts of which that at Lambley, 110 feet high with nine arches of 58-foot span each, is the biggest. Gradients are as steep as 1 in 56 in places. The line was opened throughout on 17 November 1852.

The day's travelling was completed behind 'A3' No 60101 Cicero on the 6.20pm from Newcastle (7.39pm ex-Haltwhistle), calling at Gilsland and Brampton Junction. Approaching Carlisle a glimpse of the NBR in the shape of 0-6-0 No 64526 and 0-6-2T No 69174 was had.

# SATURDAY 7-MONDAY 16 JULY 1956
# SOUTH DEVON TOUR

*D*uring my schooldays our family holidays and outings were exclusively by the Southern and Great Western railways, hence my special affection for these two companies. It was therefore with great pleasure that I was able to return to South Devon, travelling over lines of the two corresponding BR Regions, and – this time – with the added bonus of shed visits.

## SATURDAY 7 JULY 1956

No 34050 *Royal Observer Corps* was the engine on the 9.00am Waterloo-Exmouth and Sidmouth train, calling at Surbiton at 9.18am to pick up, where I joined it after travelling from Earlsfield in a Hampton Court train. For most of the journey the running was inauspicious, probably by virtue of delays from the preceding 8.54am from Waterloo to Plymouth and Ilfracombe, which makes the same stops as the 9.00am from Woking to Templecombe. This in its turn was quite possibly delayed by other main-line trains, as traffic at that time on Saturday mornings is very intensive.

Before leaving Surbiton BR 4MT 4-6-0 No 75079, transferred from Exmouth Junction to Basingstoke, was seen on an up eight-coach semi-fast.

We left Surbiton a few minutes late and called at Woking, Basingstoke, Andover, Salisbury, Templecombe and Yeovil Junction, where I alighted, about 30 minutes late. After several of the stops great difficulty was experienced in starting, a frequent trouble with the 4-6-2s, but in this case clearly due to bad handling. We did run fast west of Salisbury, however.

0-6-0D No 13011 was at Basingstoke, apparently ex-works. Several BR 4MT 2-6-0s were in evidence outside Salisbury running shed. The GWR depot there is now used for storing 'museum pieces' only, although the turntable is apparently in use.

7 July 1956: 'Battle of Britain' 4-6-2 No 34050 *Royal Observer Corps* heads the 9.00am express from Waterloo at Yeovil Junction.

7 July 1956: Chard Central, opened in 1866, was a GWR and LSWR joint station. The architecture, when seen 90 years later, is still 'early Great Western'.

From Yeovil Junction I used a stopping train to Axminster as far as Chard Junction, hauled by 'S15' No 30826. The branch to Chard Central starts from a short platform alongside the main station, and although formerly an SR line the connecting train consisted of 0-6-0PT No 3669 with two GWR non-corridor bogies, several vans and wagons and an SR brake-van. The connecting line drops sharply away round a 90-degree curve, and 3¼ miles further on makes an end-on junction with the GWR branch from Taunton, at Chard Central. This is a single-platform station with one track spanned by a Brunel timber roof, a parallel loop, a few sidings and derelict engine shed at the Taunton end.

There are six weekday trains in each direction with one extra on Saturdays, one of which stops at Ilminster only. The others call at all five stations between Taunton and Chard Central, and the journey time is from 36 to 47 minutes for the 15¼ miles.

From Taunton to Newton Abbot a Plymouth train was used. This was side-tracked at Dawlish Warren to allow the 'Torbay Express' to pass, 13 chocolate-and-cream-painted coaches, 'Castle'-hauled and running was about 20 minutes late.

During a short spell at Newton Abbot great activity was witnessed as successive westbound trains arrived, with engines changed and pilots taken on for the climb over Dainton and Rattery banks. Any motive power combination seems to be used. Two down trains had Nos 6900 + 6808 and Nos 5085 + 5089, while an up train had a 'Manor' piloting a '47XX' 2-8-0.

The journey to Torquay was completed in a Wolverhampton-Paignton train running about 10 minutes late.

### MONDAY 9 JULY 1956

Although Newton Abbot has been visited on many occasions, this is the first time the shed has been visited. It is a somewhat cramped six-road depot alongside the station, separated from the running lines by carriage sidings, and with the old works of the South Devon Railway, now used for heavy repairs, at the rear. The allocation of about 75 includes a dozen 'Castles', a few 'Halls' and 'Granges', three 'Manors' (which, with others at Plymouth Laira, perform a great deal of piloting over the Newton Abbot-Plymouth section), eight '28XX' and '38XX' 2-8-0s, a few 2-6-0s, and a large number of '51XX' 2-6-2Ts, 0-6-0PTs and 0-4-2Ts. The '45XX' tanks have been replaced in recent years to a great extent by BR 3MT 2-6-2Ts of the '82XXX' series.

84

*Above* 7 July 1956: Ready to tackle the switchback gradients ahead, 4-6-0 Nos 6900 *Albert Hall* and 6808 *Beenham Grange* await departure from Newton Abbot.

*Below* 7 July 1956: Newton Abbot shed yard is busy, with Nos 7031 *Cromwell's Castle* and 7905 *Fowey Hall* ready to take over a westbound express.

*Above* 9 July 1956: The shedmaster at Newton Abbot checks that 'Castle' No 5053 *Earl Cairns* is fit to work the 'Torbay Express'. Its neighbours are No 6933 *Butlers Hall* and 2-6-2T No 4176.

*Below* 9 July 1956: Painted green and smartened up to work a Royal Train, ex-GWR '4300' 2-6-0 No 6385 was ready for a more humdrum duty when seen at Exeter shed.

*Above* 9 July 1956: This could be the widest level crossing in the country, where 'E1R' 0-6-2Ts Nos 32124 and 32135 are seen on banking duties at Exeter St David's.

*Below* 9 July 1956: With 57 years of service to its credit, there is still work for Drummond 'T9' 4-4-0 No 30711 pictured arriving at St David's.

9 July 1956 : 'BR3' 2-6-2T No 82019 pilots '700' Class 0-6-0 No 30691 on a transfer freight from Exeter St David's to Central. Even with two locomotives at the front, this heavy freight train needs 'M7' 0-4-4T No 30669 at the rear for the climb out of St David's.

At Exeter the WR shed was visited. The allocation is almost 30, and 15 engines were on shed including 2-6-0 No 6385, painted green, and 8F 2-8-0 No 48475, one of a number on loan to the WR and operating in the West Country.

0-4-2T No 1469 on three coaches was the engine to Tiverton, and No 1468 on one modern auto-carriage thence on the 4¾- mile journey to Tiverton Junction. There is one intermediate halt, with about a dozen trains each way, the normal journey time being 12 minutes.

Tiverton Junction is a spacious station with two island platforms, the outer face of the up one being used by the Tiverton trains and of the down one by the Hemyock branch trains. There is a small single-road engine shed in the angle between the main and Tiverton lines.

The Hemyock branch curves sharply away from the down main line at the London end, climbing steeply at 1 in 66. It then pursues a sinuous course, in a generally easterly direction along the Culm Valley for a distance of 7½ miles, through Uffculme and Culmstock to Hemyock. There are two halts in addition to the stations mentioned, and the journey time varies from 35 to 57 minutes. Services consist of four down and five up trains on weekdays, with one extra train between Tiverton and Uffculme, which on Saturdays is extended to Culmstock.

The line was constructed, to the standard gauge, by the Bristol & Exeter Railway, which by the time it was opened in 1876 the GWR had taken over. It is single track throughout, with passing loops and sidings at the two stations, and a run-round loop and small goods yard at Hemyock. Passenger accommodation is provided by an elderly gas-lit Brake 3rd, and our train consisted of this plus two milk tank wagons for the dairy at Hemyock, hauled by 0-4-2T No 1435.

We returned from Tiverton Junction to Exeter in a stopping train hauled by 2-6-0 No 5344. Two more 8F 2-8-0s, Nos 48431/36, were seen while approaching Exeter.

A visit to Exmouth Junction shed showed that variety has scarcely diminished. The 40 locomotives recorded included examples of 13

9 July 1956: Hemyock, terminus of the delightful branch from Tiverton Junction. The carriage is an ex-Barry Railway 1920-built Brake 3rd.

*Above* 9 July 1956: The main source of traffic on the Hemyock branch was milk from the dairy at the terminus, hence the empty tanks that have arrived behind 0-4-2T No 1435.

*Below* 9 July 1956: Summer sunshine at Thorverton! An Exeter to Dulverton train has arrived, formed of corridor coaches of GWR and LMS design, powered by '1400' 0-4-2T No 1469.

classes, including a WR 2-6-0, an LMR 2P 2-6-2T and BR 3MT 2-6-2Ts. The SR engines included rebuilt 'Merchant Navy' 4-6-2 No 35018, two of the Lyme Regis branch Adams 4-4-2Ts, Nos 30583/84, 'O2' 0-4-4Ts, Adams 'Duplicate' 0-6-0s and an 'E1R' 0-6-2T. Two more of the latter were banking trains up from St David's to Central station.

No 82018 on a train from Exmouth hauled us from Polesloe Bridge Halt into Exeter.

No 82034 of the same class was the engine on the Torquay line portion of the 3.30pm express from Paddington, which divides at Exeter.

## THURSDAY 12 JULY 1956

The 10.38am ex-Torquay is a Paignton-Plymouth through train, non-stop from Newton Abbot. On both of the days this train was used a '41XX' worked the eight coaches to Newton Abbot and 'County' No 1021 thence to Plymouth. Departure from Torquay was delayed by an up freight that took refuge in Torre yard before we could start.

From Plymouth I travelled on the 12.12pm to Launceston, with 2-6-2T No 4583 hauling a three-coach train including two of the 'Riviera' stock corridor coaches with recessed end doors.

The Launceston branch, 32 miles long, branches off the main line at Tavistock

9 July 1956: This 'N' 2-6-0, No 31834, seen at Exmouth Junction shed, was one of 15 employed on the 'Withered Arm' lines west of Exeter at that time.

Junction, just west of the goods yard, and heads due north, climbing steadily along the western side of the thickly wooded valley of the Plym. The first station, just after leaving the main line, is Marsh Mills, beyond which there is a china clay works. 0-6-0PT No 3639 passed round the back of the up platform on a freight from this works. After Plym Bridge Halt the next station is Bickleigh, some way from the village of that name. Here the gradient is 1 in 58 and the railway crosses a high viaduct south of the station.

The River Plym forks away eastward into the heart of the moors, and the railway then follows a tributary, the River Meavy, which still heads northwards. After two more halts, Yelverton (10¼ miles from Plymouth) is reached. Here the Princetown branch, recently closed to passenger traffic, makes a trailing connection, the up platform being an island, the outer face serving the Princetown branch as it turns sharply away. There are splendid views away over the moors, the television mast on North Hessary Tor beyond Princetown being clearly seen.

0-4-2T No 1434 was passed here, on the 12.35pm Tavistock to Plymouth auto-train.

*Above* 12 July 1956: No West Country visit would be complete without a train-watching session by the coast at Dawlish. Here No 6009 *King Charles II* heads a westbound express.

*Below* 12 July 1956: Freight trains were in a minority in 'Glorious Devon' but, sandwiched in between the holiday expresses, we see 2-8-0 No 2881 at Teignmouth.

13 July 1956: Tavistock South is surely another inspiration for modellers, with water tank, lower-quadrant signal, and 2-6-2T No 4593 with train to complete the picture.

The watershed is now crossed and the gradient is then in the favour of northbound trains, and at Horrabridge the railway follows for a short distance the River Walkham, a tributary of the Tavy. Four miles further on, Tavistock is reached. Six trains from Plymouth terminate here, four more going through to Launceston.

There are no Sunday services in winter, but from early May and throughout the summer period three trains run each way between Plymouth and Tavistock.

The WR station, Tavistock South, has two platforms spanned by a timber roof, and a goods yard at the south end. The SR station is about three-quarters of a mile away, and lines pass through the town on opposite sides of the valley in which it lies, leaving it to the north on high viaducts. Thence to Lydford the WR and SR lines are in close proximity, and Lydford station has two platforms for each section, with fairly extensive exchange sidings. An SR Exeter-Plymouth train passed us here headed by the green GWR 2-6-0 No 6385.

From Lydford the GWR line turns westwards, and the remaining 12½ miles are through less interesting, though pleasant country. At Launceston the SR station is now used for all traffic, the two stations being alongside, each with a goods yard. There is a small engine shed for each Region, and SR 'N' 2-6-0 No 31830 was shunting in the SR sidings.

On the return journey No 6420 was at Tavistock on the 2.10pm (SO) from Plymouth,

and the 3.10pm Plymouth-Launceston, headed by No 5531, was crossed at Bickleigh. 0-6-0PT No 3790 was shunting at Marsh Mills.

Work has commenced on rebuilding Plymouth (North Road) station, and the track alongside No 1, the principal down platform, has been lifted while the latter is under reconstruction.

The 4.10pm express to Paddington, 1.20pm ex-Penzance, was used to Newton Abbot, and the 'King' Class engine gave a good run, unpiloted, over this difficult section.

## FRIDAY 13 JULY 1956

The 10.38am through train to Plymouth was used for the second day, and this time the offending freight train, consisting of only a few wagons with a 'Hall' as motive power, hurtled through Torquay and was clear of the line in time for us to make a punctual departure. 0-6-0PT No 5422 was seen at Newton Abbot, ex-works.

The 2.34pm SR Plymouth-Exeter train (2.25pm from Friary station) had WR 2-6-0 No 6319 in charge. At Bere Alston the Callington branch train was waiting, consisting of an LSW Brake 3rd and some vans with 'O2' 0-4-4T No 30225, at the outer face of the down island platform.

The branch was opened in 1908 and was the property of the Plymouth, Devonport & South Western Junction Railway until the latter was absorbed into the SR on 1 January 1923. This railway had three engines, 0-6-0T No 30756 *A. S. Harris* and 0-6-2Ts Nos 30757/58, *Earl of Mount Edgcumbe* and *Lord St Leven*. The former was transferred to London in 1940 but the latter two engines remained at Plymouth Friary shed until last month, for working the branch, when they were sent to Eastleigh awaiting withdrawal.

The branch is 9½ miles long, and six trains are provided each way, being allowed 41-47 minutes with five intermediate stops. There are two up and one down freights, the latter being supplemented by mixed trains when required.

The branch swings away from the main line down a 1 in 40 gradient, and performs a loop, descending steeply the while, before crossing the Tamar on a viaduct of 12 60-foot arches, 120 feet high, just before Calstock station is reached. There is a small goods yard here, which handles a respectable traffic in flowers and fruit in the appropriate seasons. From Calstock to Gunnislake (2¼ miles) the line climbs 400 feet, making a sharply curving semi-circle and emerging high above the Cornish bank of the Tamar, involving 1¼ miles at 1 in 38 and 40, after which there is an easier stretch followed by an average gradient of 1 in 52. Curves as sharp as 10 chains radius add to the difficulties of down freight trains.

Gunnislake station has an island platform and sidings and is nearly s a mile from the town. There are ample evidences of the tin mines of bygone days, in the shape of crumbling towers and chimneys half covered in vegetation. The line still climbs at grades varying from 1 in 45 to 1 in 88, and at Chilsworthy turns westwards, to face another ascent equally steep but easing before Latchley Halt is reached. Between Latchley and Luckett, the next station, there is a brief down-grade, then climbing is resumed at grades from 1 in 54 to 1 in 200 to the summit nearly 700 feet above sea level. There are undulating grades thence to Callington.

Callington station has one platform, four coaches long, the platform and track being roofed over for half that length. There is a fair-sized goods yard with seven sidings, three on one side of the line and four on the other. The loop is at the Bere Alston end of the station, where there is a small two-road shed, outside which stood LMS Ivatt 2-6-2T No 41315.

On our return to Bere Alston the 0-4-4T picked up a two-coach set of LSW 'gate stock', making a three-coach train in all, and this proved necessary when a large crowd disembarked from a Plymouth-Exeter train. I returned to Plymouth on the 11.30am Brighton-Plymouth 'West Country'-hauled 5.36pm from Bere Alston, calling at Devonport only. Here 'E1R' No 32096 was shunting while a 'West Country' waited in the up platform for the tank engine to complete its freight train.

The Plymouth-Newton Abbot journey was made behind 'Castle' No 5021, on the 7.10pm stopping train.

## SATURDAY 14 JULY 1956

At Torquay Saturday morning traffic is very heavy and trains rarely get away to time. We travelled on the 11.30am non-stop to London in 4hr 18min. A 'Hall', tender first, brought the empty stock from Newton Abbot. 'Castle' No 4089, with 11 coaches, was the train engine.

One train, passing through towards Paignton, had a 4-6-0 piloting 0-6-0 No 2230, this being an unusual class on the Kingswear line.

We left Torquay 5 minutes late, and running to Exeter, though unchecked, was restrained. We were stopped for signals at Cowley Bridge Junction at 12.15pm and suffered severe delays from a preceding train to Whitehall summit. A fast run down Wellington bank brought us through Taunton at 1.20pm, and left 148 minutes for the remaining 143 miles. Running thereafter was very good, with sustained 65-70mph. We were checked at Hungerford at 2.33, having run the 81½ miles in 73 minutes, and again at Reading West, by which time, however, we had made sufficient recovery to give us a good chance of an early arrival.

We did in fact arrive 2 minutes ahead of time, although stopped at Westbourne Park with an inevitable slow run into Paddington.

# SATURDAY 9 MARCH 1957
# TONBRIDGE

*D*ue *to the Southern Railway's concentration on electrification in the 1920s and 1930s, new construction of steam locomotives was strictly limited, thus extending the life of many pre-Grouping veterans, further prolonged by the outbreak of war. Some of these types were seen in the course of these next two journeys, particularly at Tonbridge, where both the SECR and LB&SCR were represented. A year later, when the third rail was extended to Dover and Thanet, many of them were speedily consigned to the breaker's yard.*

The 9.15am Charing Cross-Dover train hauled by 4-6-2 No 34075 made a brisk run out of London once clear of London Bridge, but was badly checked in the region of Orpington. Lengthened platforms to take ten-coach electric trains are a feature at the suburban stations out to Sevenoaks.

A visit to Tonbridge shed was rewarded by a good variety of motive power. The LBSC was represented by a 'K' 2-6-0 in resplendent condition, obviously fresh from works, a 'C2X' 0-6-0, several 'E4' 0-6-2Ts and two 'E3s', the latter in store.

SECR engines included 'L' Class 4-4-0s, 'C' Class 0-6-0s and 'H' Class 0-4-4Ts, the latter prominent in various auto-train workings towards both Tunbridge Wells and Paddock Wood. Of SR origin were 'N' and 'U1' 2-6-0s, 'Q1' 0-6-0s, 'Schools' 4-4-0s, 'Battle of Britain' 4-6-2s on the main line, and an SR-built 0-6-0 diesel shunting in the goods yard. A heavily laden train appeared from the

9 March 1957: Tonbridge shed displayed a variety of pre-Grouping motive power – this is an LB&SCR example, Class 'K' 2-6-0 No 32349.

*Left* 9 March 1957: This rather woebegone pair of 'E3' 0-6-2Ts may well have seen the end of their working lives, when discovered 'dumped' at Tonbridge shed.

*Below* 9 March 1957: Representing the South Eastern at Tonbridge shed is 'L' 4-4-0 No 31773. It was delivered from Borsig of Berlin in March 1914, shortly before the outbreak of the First World War.

direction of Ashford hauled by a 'Schools' and piloted by a 'Q1', which reappeared shortly afterwards running light down the main line. On the Hastings line rebuilt 4-4-0s and Brighton BR 2-6-4T Nos 80150/53 were seen, the latter on trains to and from Tonbridge Wells West.

We returned as far as Sevenoaks behind 'H' No 31239, which had taken over from 'L' No 31780 at Tonbridge. This loco had brought in the three-coach train after an 'all-stations' run from Hastings. At Sevenoaks we changed onto the 11.10am from Hastings, due at Charing Cross at 12.58pm, behind 'Schools' No 30917. A smart run was enjoyed, arrival at Waterloo being a minute or two before time. At Hither Green diesels Nos 13271/72/73 were all seen, these being transfers from Guildford.

# EAST GRINSTEAD

The East Grinstead-Lewes line, closed on 13 June 1955, was reopened on 7 August 1956 after a legal battle between a local resident and the Railway Executive. It now has a service of four trains daily in each direction at 2-hourly intervals. Kingscote and Barcombe stations, at the opposite ends of the line, remain closed completely, and the other stations are unstaffed with the exception of Horsted Keynes, which is the junction for a branch from Haywards Heath, and which is served by electric trains from Seaford. It is expected that as soon as the correct Parliamentary procedure can be instituted the service will be suspended.

In the course of a visit to Newick & Chailey a journey was made over most of this route, from the East Grinstead end. Services were being worked by new BR 2-6-4Ts Nos 80150/52 from Brighton shed, hauling single LBSCR carriages with side-gangway. The trains used were quite well patronised, although probably Saturday produces more traffic than weekdays.

The 10.53am Brighton slow train was used from Clapham Junction to Three Bridges, where 'H' tank No 31521 with a two-coach

LBSCR 'auto' set was waiting in the bay platform, to provide a connecting service to East Grinstead. Later on this service was shared by 'M7' 0-4-4T No 30056. Connection at East Grinstead is made with the hourly service between Victoria and Tunbridge Wells West. Several trains on this route were observed, worked by 2-6-4Ts of LMS and BR design, and 'U1' 2-6-0s. On the up trains, No 42103 worked the 12.25pm (11.47am ex-Tunbridge Wells West) and was later seen returning on the 3.08pm ex-Victoria. No 80016 worked the 2.25pm and No 42068 the 3.25pm, on which we travelled with a train consisting of three Bulleid coaches. No 31908 arrived on the 2.08pm from Victoria and another 'U1', No 31896, was passed at Sanderstead on the 3.38pm ex-Victoria (Saturdays only) with through carriages to Eastbourne. At Oxted 'H' 0-4-4T No 31177 was seen on the shuttle service to Tunbridge Wells via Edenbridge.

16 March 1957: BR Class 4 2-6-4T No 80016 heads a Victoria train at East Grinstead (High Level). The station below was on the Three Bridges to Tunbridge Wells line.

# SATURDAY 5 OCTOBER 1957
# HITCHIN

*When re-reading my notes on this Saturday outing I was reminded of what one of our contemporary enthusiasts' magazines aptly describes as the 'Glorious Years'. In just 2 hours I recorded 40 locomotives – probably ten times as many as one would see at a busy junction today – and all but one were steam!*

Unlike the occasion earlier in the year when a visit was made to Hitchin for photographic purposes, bright sunshine enabled a number of negatives to be secured, while traffic was brisk and interesting.

The down journey was made on the 10.45am buffet car express to Grantham, calling at Hatfield only, hauled by a 'V2', and the return journey on the Cambridge-King's Cross semi-fast train hauled by 'V2' No 60983. Over 40 engines were recorded during

5 October 1957: A Cambridge to King's Cross buffet car express hauled by 'B1' 4-6-0 No 61094 calls at Hitchin.

the 2-hour stay, about half of which were either already in the shed yard or went on shed at the termination of their duties. In the former category were 'A4' No 60003 *Andrew K. McCosh* and 'A3' No 60044 *Melton*, which had failed, 'V2' No 60864 (50A), which had probably also failed, and an unidentified 'M of S' 2-8-0 minus pony-truck. On shed in the course of normal duties were BR 9F 2-10-0 No 92141 from New England, and an assortment of 'B1s', 'L1s', 'J6s', 'J15' No 65479 and a 'J69'. Other engines of classes 'B1', 'B17', 'L1', 'N2', 'J6', 'J69' and 'M of S' 2-8-0 came on shed from traffic.

Of particular interest was 'J69' No 68654, which brought in the RAF leave train from Henlow in place of the 'J15' mentioned. The train consisted of two four-coach 'articulateds' and was taken on to London by a 'V2'. An up excursion from the Sheffield area came past about 11.50am behind 'A3' No 60067 and another from Chesterfield behind 'B1' No 61185 (38A), presumably in connection with the Nottingham Forest v Spurs match.

The 'pièce de resistance' was York 'BR5' No 73167 on the 12.21pm King's Cross-Cambridge semi-fast. Main-line expresses seen included the 9.15am York-King's Cross headed by 'W1' 4-6-4 No 60700, the 11.50am down 'Queen of Scots' behind 'A1' No 60133, another 'A1', No 60135, on the 8.00am Newcastle-King's Cross, 'A4' No 60025 on the express due at King's Cross at 1.39pm with through coaches from Sunderland, 'A2' No 60533 on the 12.30pm down 'Northumbrian', No 60500 on the 1.00pm 'Heart of Midlothian' (King's Cross-Perth), and 'A3' No 60102 on the 10.00am Leeds-London.

An 0-6-0 diesel, D3441, 'ex-works', was included in an up freight train.

*Above* 5 October 1957: A up special for Sheffield United supporters races through Hitchin, hopefully in time for the kick-off. Doing the honours is 'A3' 4-6-2 No 60067 *Ladas*.

*Below* 5 October 1957: As a contrast to the 'Pacifics' on expresses, ex-GER 'J68' 0-6-0T No 68654 arrives at Hitchin with a pair of 'quad-art' sets, forming an RAF leave train from Henlow camp.

# WATFORD AND STRATFORD

*T*he stream of 'specials' on Wembley Cup Final days fully justified these trips out of Euston on the 'North Western' main line, with Watford shed as an added attraction. The several types of LMS-built 4-6-0s almost monopolised haulage of the specials, and on such busy days freight traffic was inevitably conspicuous by its absence. After so many years I can't remember what prompted a diversion to Stratford – possibly a surfeit of 'Black Fives' and 'Jubilees'?

No 46119 hauled the 10.50am down Llandudno and Blackpool express, and diesel No 10001 the 1.42pm up from Watford, a semi-fast train that was delayed by the pressure of special traffic.

With Bolton Wanderers and Manchester United in the Cup Final, the Western Division of the LMR bore the brunt of the special traffic. An endless stream of trains arrived from early morning until about 2pm, terminating at Wembley as kick-off time drew nearer. The posters displayed at Euston showed return workings commencing soon after 6pm and becoming intensive between 10pm and midnight, with the last train soon after 1.00am.

3 May 1958: A fine sight at Watford, as 8P 4-6-2 No 46239 *City of Chester* hurries through with the 'Ulster Express' from Heysham to Euston.

Variety of motive power was, of course, strictly limited. The majority of trains were powered by Class 5s with a few 'Scots', one 'Jubilee' and one 'Britannia' being seen. The regular long-distance trains, of course, produced LMR 'Pacifics' and 'Patriots' in addition. A shuttle service between Euston and Wembley Central had Fowler 2-6-4Ts as motive power.

Engines seen included Nos 44690/96, 44742/49/69, 44819 (17A), 44773, 44831, 45278/43, 45305/08/69, 45493, 45587, 45706, 46101/54/11 and 70033. The up 'Shamrock' had No 44768 piloting 46142, the 'Mancunian' had No 46153 and the 'Ulster Express' No 46239.

A brief visit to Stratford showed LMR 2-6-0 No 43108 outside the Old Works and No 43144 near the works locomotive shed.

3 May 1958: 'Rebuilt Scot' No 46119 *Lancashire Fusilier* starts northbound from Watford with a Blackpool and Llandudno express.

3 May 1958: With only 17 miles to go, the hard work is nearly over for the crew of 7P 4-6-0 No 46153 *The Royal Dragoon* passing Watford on the up 'Mancunian'.

*Above* 3 May 1958: This Saturday was Cup Final day, so it was the expectation of seeing the 'specials' that lured me to Watford. This one, for Manchester United fans, is hauled by 'Jubilee' 4-6-0 No 45706 *Express*.

*Below* 3 May 1958: Not all the Cup Final 'specials' were entrusted to named locomotives. This one, by way of a change, has 'Caprotti' Class 5 4-6-0 No 44769.

*Above* 3 May 1958: Contrasting with the heavy activity on the main line on Cup Final day, all is peaceful on Watford shed, with 3P 2-6-2T No 40010, a 'BR4' 2-6-4T and a 4F 0-6-0 resting between duties.

*Below* 3 May 1958: My session at Watford was followed by a trip to Stratford, where I recorded Class 4 2-6-0 No 43108 outside the Old Works, and 'N7' 0-6-2T No 69721 on a train from Hertford.

# A KENTISH CONTRAST: ASHFORD AND THE RH&DR

*During this day I made my first visit to the 15-inch-gauge Romney, Hythe & Dymchurch Railway – still happily with us today – and in consequence was able to enjoy runs behind 'Pacific' locomotives on both the standard and narrow gauge. En route, the New Romney branch was 'new track' and the visit to Ashford shed produced 16 classes of steam and two of diesel locomotives.*

The 9.09am Charing Cross-Dover and Ramsgate express is allowed 80 minutes for the 56 miles to Ashford with stops at Waterloo, Sevenoaks and Tonbridge. This schedule allows for a severe PW restriction at Chislehurst where the flying and burrowing junctions with the Victoria-Chatham main line are being extensively relaid in readiness for electrification.

Rebuilt 'West Country' 4-6-2 No 34026 *Yes Tor* kept the schedule with ease, although running as far as Sevenoaks was restrained throughout with no attempt at high speeds. Smart work from Hildenborough down to Tonbridge, and sustained high speed thence to the approaches to Ashford, more than regained any lost time.

The rebuilding of 'West Country' engines for the Eastern Section goes on apace, and several were seen on principal trains. Passing Hither Green pre-war 0-6-0 diesel No 15202 appeared to be out of service on a siding alongside the shed. Several SR and BR types were, as usual, at work in the yards, and an LMR 'Jinty' on transfer freight duties was also in evidence in the shed yard.

At Ashford local passenger duties are shared by a variety of types. The LMR 2-6-4Ts are extensively used on Maidstone East and Dover trains, with BR and LMR Class 2 2-6-2Ts on those through Canterbury West to Ramsgate. 4-4-0s of the 'Schools' and 'L1' Classes are much in evidence also.

One particular object of the day's expedition was to travel for the first time on the Romney, Hythe & Dymchurch Railway. A glimpse of the station and some rolling stock at Hythe a few years ago, deserted during the mid-winter, and a view of 4-6-2 No 10 *Winston Churchill* on display at Waterloo in 1948, were the only previous contacts with the line.

The railway is 15 miles in length, the principal station, with three platform roads, a covered roof, a turntable and sidings, being at Hythe. The route follows close to the coast through Dymchurch to New Romney and on across an expanse of shingle to Dungeness, where a return loop avoids reversal. The line is double between Hythe and New Romney, the headquarters, where there is a three-road locomotive shed, a workshop and an extensive carriage shed. The station has two through staggered platforms and a terminal bay facing Hythe. There are several intermediate stations and halts, all with adequate and substantial shelters, several being adjacent to holiday camps, which provide a good deal of traffic.

The basic service as commencing in mid-April consists of four through trains in each direction and four each way between Hythe and New Romney. Some of these latter continue as far as Maddieson's Camp as and when required. The service gradually increases as the summer season approaches, and in the height of the holiday season there are numerous special and extra trains.

*Above* 17 May 1958: Although Gresley never designed a 4-8-2, this splendid 15-inch-gauge one on the RH&DR gives us some idea what it would have looked like. No 5 *Hercules* is seen at Hythe.

*Below* 17 May 1958: This smart little RH&DR 'Pacific', No 3 *Southern Maid*, is a Davey Paxman product of 1926, and is heading a Hythe to Dungeness train at New Romney.

The motive power consists of nine steam engines – seven 'Pacifics' and two 4-8-2s. Five of the 'Pacifics' are faithful reproductions of the original Gresley 'A1s', while the other two are of American outline. These all have 2ft 1½in driving wheels, while the 4-8-2s, also of typical 'Gresley' appearance, have 1ft 7½in wheels. All have two cylinders, 5¼in by 7½in, but two of the 'Gresley' 4-6-2s originally had three cylinders of this size. The 'American' 4-6-2s are the most recent acquisitions, having been built in 1931, the 'Gresley' 4-6-2s in 1925/27 and the 4-8-2s in 1927. The 'American' engines were built by the Yorkshire Engine Co Ltd and the remainder by Davey Paxman of Colchester. One of the 4-6-2s, No 8 *Hurricane*, is fitted with a bogie 'corridor' tender. This engine is painted blue, but most of the remainder are now a yellow-brown reminiscent of the North British Railway. There are also a couple of petrol engines with Rolls-Royce motors. One of these, a four-wheeled vehicle, was in a siding at Dymchurch.

Rolling stock consists of over 50 bogie passenger vehicles, mostly fitted with roller bearings and seating eight people in two compartments. These are painted blue below the waistline and white above, and are of several variations of outward appearance. There are also some 16-seat open vehicles for use in suitable weather, and a number of ballast wagons.

The line was opened between New Romney and Hythe in July 1927 and the extension to Dungeness was completed in 1929. The station here is of a very simple type with one platform and a siding, and is within 100 yards of the lighthouse.

We travelled from Hythe to Dungeness in the 12.20pm train, returning from Dungeness to New Romney at 2.00pm. Seventy minutes are allowed for the 15 miles, inclusive of stops, that at New Romney being of 5 minutes duration. Our engine throughout was 4-8-2 No 5 *Hercules*. We passed 4-6-2 No 3 *Southern Maid* near Dymchurch and 4-8-2 No 6 *Samson* at New Romney. The shed there housed 4-6-2 Nos 1 *Green Goddess*, 2 *Northern Chief* and 8 *Hurricane*. The two 'American'-type engines, Nos 9 *Doctor Syn* and 10 *Winston Churchill*,

17 May 1958: New Romney & Littlestone on Sea was a branch line terminus on the former SE&CR. 'H' 0-4-4T No 31522 is depicted there on an Ashford train.

17 May 1958: Nearest in this line of tank engines in Ashford shed yard is 'Z' 0-8-0T No 30952. Next is an Ivatt Class 2 2-6-2T, with another 'Z' at the rear.

were stored in the carriage shed (No 10 partially dismantled). The only engine not seen was No 7 *Typhoon*, which, it was understood, was being completely rebuilt in the workshops.

At New Romney the SR standard-gauge station is adjacent to the RH&DR depot. 'H' 0-4-4T No 31522 was waiting on the 3.01pm train to Ashford, consisting of an SECR two-coach set. The branch leaves the Ashford-Hastings route at Appledore, and between Lydd Town and Lydd-on-Sea makes almost a 180-degree turn to run due north, to New Romney. There are no signs now of the derelict branch to Dungeness, save the rotting remnants of the small station shelter and platform at the latter. There are eight down and nine up trains, a few of which start and terminate at Appledore, the remainder running through to and from Ashford.

A visit to Ashford shed produced a list of 50 locomotives of no fewer than 17 different classes!

The return journey from Ashford was made on the 5.10pm non-stop to Waterloo with a schedule of 68 minutes. This was kept with ease, notwithstanding a cautious approach to Tonbridge, the slack at Chislehurst and a signal check at Hither Green. The same engine as on the outward journey, No 34026, was responsible.

# SATURDAY 31 MAY 1958

# LINCOLNSHIRE AND NOTTINGHAMSHIRE

*I shudder to think what this 300-mile round trip would cost today, especially as all the tickets were booked 'on the spot', but I certainly felt it well worth while at the time, if only for the variety of steam haulage over most of the route. The 'mile-a-minute' averages on the run back to St Pancras made a fitting conclusion to a day full of interest.*

A round trip of over 300 miles was accomplished in precisely 12 hours, inclusive of walks to and from Clapham Junction, 1¼ hours at Peterborough, half an hour at Lincoln and 2 hours at Nottingham. Weather varied from hot sunshine to heavy rain, and a good combination of locomotive recording, new mileage and photography was enjoyed.

From King's Cross to Peterborough the 10.05am relief train to Glasgow was used. This had 'V2' No 60862 on a modest load, and some very fast running was experienced after a late start of about 5 minutes.

The GN main line was busy with several excursions following each other, 'B1'-hauled. An up express passed near Hatfield hauled by a large diesel locomotive, presumably D201, which is on trials from Hornsey depot.

The steady spread of diesel motive power to depots in the '34 area' (now embracing Peterborough) was marked by the recording of 200hp engines at Hatfield and Hitchin as well as by the replacement of 'J50' and 'J52' engines by 350hp diesels on shunting duties in the Finsbury Park neighbourhood.

At Peterborough a succession of long-distance expresses in both directions was taxing the limited capacity of the station, and delays were mounting. A boat train for Tyne Commission Quay, headed by 'V2' 2-6-2 No 60800 *Green Arrow*, was hard at the heels of the 10.10am Glasgow train hauled by 'A4' No 60020, and the 10.20am Leeds and Bradford finally got away, after much slipping, about 30 minutes late.

The GNR 'C12' 4-4-2Ts, which have been a familiar sight for so many years on station pilot duties, have now been scrapped and replaced by 'N5' 0-6-2Ts. No 69262 (formerly of Chester Northgate) was one of these, sharing shunting duties at the south end with two diesels.

The 12.12pm Peterborough-Cleethorpes, a three-car diesel set, left about 20 minutes late, delayed by the lateness of the main-line trains, but regained a few minutes by brisk running. At Spalding several of the LMR 2-6-0s and 'J6' 0-6-0s were around the shed, with a 'J69' 0-6-0T and diesel No 11160. Formerly a sub-depot to Peterborough, Spalding is now under the control of Boston, and provides motive power for trains on the M&GN route, which crosses the GN route at right-angles.

From Werrington Junction to the outskirts of Boston the line is practically dead straight and level. Boston is a junction where routes westward to Grantham, and north-westward to Lincoln, leave the Peterborough-Grimsby route.

I changed here onto the 1.14pm to Lincoln, a six-car diesel train, which started from a bay platform. On the up platform a Grantham-bound diesel train was waiting, striking evidence of the extent of the modernisation plan in this part of the country. As further evidence, 0-6-0D Nos 11178/79/86 stood in the goods sidings south of the station.

It is 31 miles to Lincoln, and the current winter timetable gives seven through trains daily. There are four more trains from Skegness, which join the route at Woodhall Junction, and five in the opposite direction. Our train continued to Sheffield after a wait at Lincoln, and although it is not clear from the timetable, it would appear that several do so. Journey time between Boston and Lincoln is between 55 and 70 minutes, according to the number of stops made.

From Woodhall Junction there is a branch to Horncastle, closed to passenger traffic in September 1954, and from Bardney a line to Louth, closed in November 1951. A freight was waiting on this line headed by Doncaster 2-10-0 No 92171. Thence to the outskirts of Lincoln the railway is paralleled on both sides by waterways, so that the only access to Five Mile House station is via the bridges over these.

Lincoln is a traffic centre of considerable importance and complexity, approached from eight directions by ex-GN, GN & GE Joint, GC

*31 May 1958: Class 'B16/3' 4-6-0 No 61448 sets off from Lincoln station for the shed, after arriving on a train from York.*

and Midland railways. Of these, the Midland route, from Nottingham, uses the separate St Marks station. The Central station approach tracks are crossed on the level by roads at either end, causing great congestion to road traffic, but a concrete road viaduct is under construction at the eastern end. A diesel railcar depot has been built alongside the Boston-Lincoln line, since most local services radiating from the city are now worked by these vehicles.

By contrast to the size and activity of Central station, St Marks presents a distinctly woebegone appearance. The two platforms enclose four tracks, the centre pair being carriage sidings, and sidings at the back of the station cross the main road to link up with Eastern Region tracks. There are 12 services each way between Lincoln and Nottingham on weekdays, nearly all diesel-worked. Several start or terminate at Derby, and one is a through train between Birmingham and Cleethorpes. Several are 'all stations', the others omit some or most stops, particularly between Rolleston Junction and Nottingham in the case of Derby trains. An eastbound working leaving Nottingham at 3.57am calls at Newark only and is a mail train, which does

not appear to have any counterpart in the opposite direction. Journey times vary from 50 to 80 minutes for 31 miles.

At Newark the GN main line is crossed on the level and there is a connection between the two routes. The Midland station is small with very short platforms, but there are a number of goods sidings.

Four miles further on at Rolleston Junction, a line branches off to Mansfield. This has a passenger service as far as Southwell, the first station, a distance of 2½ miles. It is worked by two MR 0-4-4Ts stationed at Newark, and there are 13 down and 15 up trains on weekdays (16 each way on Saturdays), most of which run through to or from Newark. No 58085 was so engaged on this occasion.

Approaching Nottingham the line passes under the former LNER lines in the neighbourhood of Colwick, and joins the route from Melton Mowbray immediately before entering Nottingham (Midland) station.

Our train was worked by 'D16/3' 4-4-0 No 62599, a class that has recently replaced 'Director' 'D11' Class engines on this service.

Traffic was busy during nearly 2 hours at Nottingham, with diesel railcars working services in the Lincoln, Derby and Leicester directions. All trains to and from Mansfield and Worksop are still steam-hauled, by 2P 4-4-0s, Class 2 2-6-0s and 2-6-4Ts. The usual variety of 4F 0-6-0s, 8F and an 'M of S' 2-8-0s, were working freight trains on the avoiding lines at the back of the station. Long-distance expresses to and from London and destinations beyond Nottingham use the Melton Mowbray route, avoiding Leicester and eliminating the necessity for reversal at Nottingham. Since accelerations came into force many of these trains are double-headed, with a 'Jubilee' or Class 5 4-6-0 piloted by an elderly 2P 4-4-0.

One such train was used for the journey to London, the Edinburgh-St Pancras 'Waverley' express, 5.45pm off Nottingham, due into London at 7.50pm – 125 minutes for 123 miles. It was reported 11 minutes late leaving Sheffield, 10 late off Chesterfield, and came into Nottingham about 5 minutes down with

31 May 1958: A 'stranger in the camp' at Nottingham Midland – ex-LNER 'D16/3' No 62599, with its train of LMS stock, is en route from Lincoln to Derby.

31 May 1958: Ivatt Class 2 2-6-0 No 46501 approaches Nottingham (Midland) with a Mansfield train.

nine coaches behind 'Compound' No 41143 piloting 'Jubilee' No 45585. The 4-minute allowance in the station was exceeded by 2 minutes, so we left 7 minutes late.

Some spirited running was enjoyed on the Nottingham-Kettering section, with a check before that station and a slowing to about 25mph to cross onto the fast roads at the London end. North of Bedford, at Oakley

Junction, there was a bad slowing to about 15mph, and the running thence to St Albans seemed to have lost its zest. Things improved thereafter right to Kentish Town, but we had lost a few minutes on this very exacting schedule, and a dead stand at Dock Junction resulted in an arrival 15 minutes late.

Passing Stewarts & Lloyds at Corby, 0-6-0ST Nos 7/10/20 were seen. The usual collection of 2-10-0s, 8Fs and 4Fs were at work on mineral trains and, to round off the excursion, Holbeck Class 5 No 44826 was noted in St Pancras.

# SATURDAY 13 SEPTEMBER 1958
# NORFOLK

*Perhaps with a foreboding that many of the network of lines in East Anglia might not remain open much longer, I made a series of visits to the area in 1958. On this day all my trains were diesel-powered, but I was still just in time to record some Great Eastern veterans going about their lawful duties.*

This third and last of a series of visits to East Anglia has accomplished coverage of most sections of route in a large area that was hitherto seriously neglected. Total mileage, inclusive of LT journeys to and from Liverpool Street, has been approximately 1,000, of which about 263, or around 27%, are new. Sections still to be dealt with are the Saxmundham-Aldeburgh, North Walsham-Mundesley, Yarmouth (South Town)-Lowestoft and Kings Lynn-Hunstanton branches. It is of course significant that of 30 locos recorded, 25 were diesel. Equally so is the fact that six trains used on this latest tour were diesel-powered. The Great Eastern line at the moment is in the vanguard of the BR modernisation plan, with Stratford, the largest MPD in Britain, scheduled to become all-diesel, and electrification forging ahead on several main and suburban routes simultaneously.

On this occasion the 9.30am ex-Liverpool Street had D203, and the 50-minute timing for the 46¾ miles from Ipswich to Norwich was improved on by 3 or 4 minutes. The 0-6-0DM at Colchester, No 11138, is nominally a Parkeston engine.

From Norwich to Wells a two-car diesel set,

13 September 1958: A 'Derby Lightweight' two-car DMU forms the 1.40pm from Wells-next-the-Sea to Norwich.

13 September 1958: Shunting a few wagons is child's play for this massive 'J19/2' 0-6-0 No 64644 in the yard at Wells-next-the-Sea.

the 12.11pm ex-Norwich, was well filled. Although most passengers detrained at intermediate stations, a good few joined, to give a respectable load throughout. The Ipswich route is left at Trowse Junction. Here three 0-6-0s ('J39' Nos 64802/82 and a 'J19') are in store. The Ely and Cambridge route is then followed to Wymondham, and we passed two eastbound steam trains on this section. At Wymondham the Wells line swings sharply northwards immediately beyond the station. There are 11 down and 10 up trains, journey time being between 81 and 105 minutes (the latter including a 20-minute stop at Dereham), with 13 intermediate stations for a 48¼ mile journey. A connection is made at Dereham with Kings Lynn trains – there are in fact three Norwich-Kings Lynn trains daily, reversing at Dereham, where the station is north of a triangle junction.

Dereham station has two through platforms, and a bay for the Kings Lynn trains. There is a sizeable goods yard and a small two-road shed now used by diesel shunters. 'J17' No 65544 and 0-6-0DM No 11165 were shunting, and an

'N7' 0-6-2T passed through later on a northbound parcels train.

Six miles beyond Dereham, at County School, there was formerly a cross-county line to Wroxham, and the up platform is an island, of which the outer face was formerly used by this service. The passenger service was discontinued several years ago and the centre section is now completely closed, there being freight services from either end.

At Fakenham the M&GN main line is crossed, and after two more intermediate stations the terminus is reached. This has two platforms flanking one track, another track on the outer face of the platforms and a short bay at the outer end of the other. There are a number of sidings and a turntable, and 'J19' No 64644 was in the yard on the branch freight. The country served by the branch is pleasant and slightly undulating, tending to become more open and barren as the coast is reached.

I returned as far as Dereham on the same train, the 1.46pm ex-Wells. The train used thence to Kings Lynn was the 2.13pm ex-Norwich (2.55-3.00pm at Dereham).

The Dereham-Lynn line is single throughout and was opened in stages between October 1846 and September 1848. There are 12 daily services each way, taking an average 58

13 September 1958: A badly-timed click of the shutter results in a lamp-post protruding from the chimney of 'D16/3' No 62606 as it arrives at Kings Lynn!

13 September 1958: Dieselisation comes to East Anglia in the shape of Brush Type 2 No D5503, seen approaching Thetford en route from Norwich to Liverpool Street via Cambridge.

minutes for 26½ miles with seven intermediate stations, and connecting in several cases with Thetford trains at Swaffham. The latter is the most important station en route, the town having a population of 3,000. The other places are all small villages.

'J17' No 65544 worked a Dereham-Lynn freight, passed on the return journey, and Nos 64658 and 68542 were at Middleton Towers, whence there are three daily trains from the sidings of British Industrial Sands Ltd, which are worked through Lynn to March and thence to Bawtry and other northern destinations. At Swaffham there are grain hoppers, which provide loads for a number of grain wagons that occupied the sidings there.

Engines seen around Kings Lynn station and loco depot were of Classes 'D16/3', 'J17', 'N7' and 'J67', No 68499 of the latter class being apparently out of service in the shed yard. 0-6-0DM Nos

D2011/13/14 were also seen, so it would appear that Nos D2011-15 are here.

Returning by the 4.12pm from Kings Lynn as far as Swaffham, another two-car diesel set was joined for the 4.50pm to Thetford. This route is 22¾ miles long, the Norwich-Ely line being joined at Roudham Junction, about 2½ miles from Thetford. There are five trains from Thetford to Swaffham, one of which continues to Dereham, and six in the opposite direction. Journey time is around 41 minutes with four intermediate stops.

At Thetford the 5.10pm Norwich-Liverpool Street was joined. This calls at Thetford at 6.03pm and makes seven stops, including Ely (12 minutes) and Cambridge (8 minutes), arriving at Liverpool Street at 8.41pm. No D5503 was responsible and, after very slow running in from Tottenham, was about 10 minutes late.

At the sugar beet factory at Ely two R&H 0-4-0Ds and a derelict 0-6-0ST were seen.

In the new yards north of Cambridge a departmental 0-6-0DM and an 0-4-0 Sentinel could be seen but not identified.

# WELLINGBOROUGH AND HIGHAM FERRERS

*T*his being a Bank Holiday Monday there was no freight activity on
the normally busy Midland main line, but by way of compensation
*I found a full complement of locos in Wellingborough's roundhouses.
The absence of a permit was no hindrance as there was not a soul to be
seen, enabling me to record the 50 or so residents in peace.*

**B**eing Whit Monday no freight trains were running and a slightly modified passenger service was in operation, with a few cancellations during the day – chiefly business services – and a number of relief trains in the evening.

In the down direction the 11.15am St Pancras-Leicester semi-fast was used, with a 93-minute schedule allowed for the 65 miles to Wellingborough, inclusive of four intermediate stops. A Class 5 was in charge, with eight coaches.

The Higham Ferrers branch leaves the main line about half a mile south of Wellingborough, and makes a sweeping curve towards the east. It is single track, with one intermediate station at Rushden (3¾ miles), where there are several goods sidings. This is a manufacturing town considerably larger than Higham Ferrers.

A two-coach set powered by a 'BR2' 2-6-2T

18 May 1959: There were only 30 BR Class 2 2-6-2Ts, so it was pleasing to find No 84007 heading my train from Wellingborough to Higham Ferrers.

*Above* 18 May 1959: Wellingborough shed was home to the ten Franco-Crosti variants of the BR 9F 2-10-0, and the 'pre-heater' can be clearly seen on No 92021.

*Below* 18 May 1959: It is 'all quiet' at Wellingborough shed on this Whit Monday; 'Crab' 2-6-0 No 42792 is stabled with an 8F 2-8-0 and a 9F 2-10-0.

18 May 1959: My Whit Monday outing on the Midland main line came to a successful conclusion when brand-new 'Metrovick' Co-Bo diesel No D5716 hauled me home from Bedford (seen here) to St Pancras.

provides the services. There are 12 down and 13 up trains on weekdays, with extras on Saturdays, journey time varying between 10 and 20 minutes according to the duration of the stop at Rushden. My train was hauled by No 84007.

Like many others, the branch is threatened with closure, since Wellingborough station is some distance from the centre of the town and buses have captured most of the traffic.

Wellingborough shed has two roundhouses and provides motive power for the main-line and local freight traffic, the only passenger engines being three 2-6-2Ts for the Higham Ferrers and Northampton services. The bulk of the allocation is made up of 9F 2-10-0s and 8F 2-8-0s, with some 4Fs, a few 0-6-0DE and 0-6-0T shunters. There were 25 2-10-0s and about a dozen 8F 2-8-0s on shed. Of interest were an ER 'O1' 2-8-0, No 63742 (41A) and a 'V2'

2-6-2, No 60879, resulting from the absorption of the former GC main line into the LM Region. A 2F 0-6-0, No 58215, and a 4F 0-6-0, No 44175, were in store, as were several of the Franco-Crosti batch of 2-10-0s, which are presumably not an unqualified success.

I returned as far as Bedford in a Kettering-Bedford stopping train (2.57pm ex-Wellingborough) hauled by 2-6-0 No 46404, and from Bedford in the 12.35pm Leeds-London express, non-stop from Bedford, departing at 4.12pm and due at St Pancras at 5.05pm. With new 1200hp 'ML2' diesel-electric No D5716, 3 minutes were cut from the schedule, an early arrival being made.

# WEST MIDLANDS AND WIRRAL

*This four-day tour of the West Midlands, Shropshire and Wirral covered 625 miles of rail travel, but produced only a modest total of 43 'cops', many of them diesel shunters. Of the five sheds visited, Birkenhead was the biggest, with 16 roads and a mixed allocation some 80 strong. In the course of my journeys I made use of steam, diesel and electric traction.*

The object of this tour was the coverage of practically all WR mileage in the Worcester/Stourbridge/Shrewsbury area not previously travelled over, including lines threatened with imminent closure. For the purpose of loco shed visits this was extended to Birkenhead. A total of 31 trains were used, of which 19 were steam-hauled, ten were diesel railcars and two (between Rock Ferry and Birkenhead) were in multiple-unit electrics. Several of the diesel journeys were in WR railcars, the remainder (mostly in the Birmingham area) in BR railcars. Generally, timekeeping was good, and all connections were maintained.

## SATURDAY 29 AUGUST 1959

The 9.45am from Paddington to Worcester lost about 20 minutes on the London-Reading stage, but on leaving the latter station it was necessary to cross to the down slow line and back across in consequence of a '61XX' 2-6-2T, which was derailed just beyond the platforms and was presumably responsible for the delay. Smart running beyond Reading regained much of the lost time, notwithstanding a lengthy stop at Evesham.

There are two BR '78XXX' 2-6-0s sub-shedded at Kingham, of which No 78008 was outside the small shed. Three '22XX' 0-6-0s were in the vicinity of Honeybourne, where the Birmingham-Cheltenham line is crossed at right-angles and where a good deal of work is in progress to improve the junctions between the two routes. At Evesham the engine shed itself was deserted but a couple of locos were shunting in the yards.

During a wait of about 20 minutes at Worcester, the most interesting engine seen was No 92109 of Leicester, which came in on a North to West passenger train of LNER stock, the engine presumably having worked from Birmingham.

The 1.10pm Worcester-Wolverhampton train consisted of five non-corridor coaches hauled by 2-6-2T No 4152. The junction for the Severn Valley line is at Hartlebury, 11¼ miles from Worcester. Here a green-painted WR diesel railcar was waiting in a siding, and we left punctually in it at 1.50pm on the 40¾-mile journey, for which 2hr 1min is allowed with 16 intermediate stops. For much of the route a good complement of passengers was carried. This is quite an attractive journey from the scenic point of view, with the river always near at hand, winding between wooded hills and with moderate-sized towns such as Bridgnorth and Ironbridge to give added interest.

The first place of consequence is Bewdley, 5½ miles from Hartlebury, where the Kidderminster-Woofferton route is crossed. There is a lengthy island platform for eastbound trains and a shorter single platform, at which we stopped, for westbound ones. Ultimately there were three WR railcars in the station at the same time, while a '43XX' 2-6-0 waited in the loop with a westbound freight train. There are no more junctions until Buildwas is reached, the numerous intermediate stops being at small halts or conventional stations with two platforms. A 3-minute stop was allowed at Bridgnorth, and here we passed the Shrewsbury-Hartlebury train consisting of two coaches hauled by 0-6-0PT No 3769 (84G).

Buildwas is the junction for the Wellington-Much Wenlock line, there being a separate single platform for the latter, higher than, and at an angle to, the Shrewsbury route There is a large power station here, and some goods sidings.

We were held waiting outside Shrewsbury until a train for the Welshpool line passed the junction, and we then moved slowly past Coleham sheds and into the station a few minutes late.

Being a summer Saturday a heavy traffic was being handled and I left for Crewe on a Manchester train, which exchanged its 'Hall' for 4-6-0 No 44986. A fast non-stop run was made, past Whitchurch, junction for the Oswestry line and for a 'goods only' route to Chester, and past Nantwich, junction for Wellington.

We were stopped near Crewe South shed before being allowed into Crewe station, where great strides have been made with preparations for the Euston-Crewe-Manchester electrification. The whole station is a mass of gantries from which the overhead cables are now being slung, and the once familiar overbridge leading to the North shed is no more. Progress is also being made in the rebuilding of that shed, where a ferro-concrete roundhouse is under construction.

The 5.12pm Crewe-Llandudno train left from a bay platform at the north end of the station, hauled by 4-6-0 No 75012. Passing Crewe Works, the last Webb tank engine, 0-6-2T No 58926, withdrawn in November 1958, could be glimpsed outside the cutting-up shop.

Chester station remains unaltered since our visits to that area in 1950 and 1951. There are four long through platforms and bay platforms, with through lines between the platform roads and alongside the station. WR trains between Shrewsbury and Birkenhead reverse in one of the bays at the north end. On summer weekends traffic is extremely heavy thanks to the incessant flow of trains serving the North Wales holiday resorts.

The WR shed has lost some of its importance, but this was hardly apparent from the lines of engines of all types visible in the yard. The LMR depot has a number of BR Standard engines on the allocation, Class 4 and 5 4-6-0s and 2-6-4Ts, while the first diesels have just arrived.

In the evening a triangular journey was made to cover the Hooton-Helsby line, leaving Chester for Hooton at 7.03pm behind a BR Class 3 2-6-2T, one of several stationed at the WR shed. The train was crowded, and was closely followed by other trains not shown in the public timetable. My train from Hooton, of six coaches hauled by 2-6-4T No 42599, waited for these and was late in starting as a result.

The most important source of traffic on the 8¾- mile Hooton-Helsby section is the enormous oil refinery at Ellesmere Port, which is served by extensive sidings. Hard by the station of that name is a two-road engine shed, which housed about four industrial locomotives. This is the ex-LNW shed now owned by the Manchester Ship Canal Co. One of the 'M of S' 0-6-0ST types was MSC 87. There was a similar shed not far away beyond the station. One of the new diesels allocated to Chester (6A), No D3764, was also in the sidings here. An oil tank train headed by an 8F 2-8-0 followed us from Stanlow. There is a triangle junction at Helsby giving direct access to the refineries from Chester.

The last stage of the day's travels was in a Manchester-Chester train hauled by 'Patriot' No 45518.

## SUNDAY 30 AUGUST 1959

Sunday was devoted to sheds, the depots concerned not having been visited for some years (Birkenhead in May 1954, Wrexham in June 1950).

The first call was at Chester Northgate, where the seven engines seen represented six classes! They were 'BR2' 2-6-2T No 84001, LMR 2-6-2T Nos 41216/25, LMR Class 3 2-6-2T No 40205, LMR Class 4 2-6-4T No 42417, LMR 0-6-0DE No 12037 and ER 'O1' 2-8-0 No 63641. A diesel railcar set was stabled in Northgate terminus station.

*Left* 30 August 1959: The small shed at Chester Northgate was home to only ten locomotives. On my visit there I found this one, 3P 2-6-2T No 40205, nicely positioned for a photograph.

*Below* 30 August 1959: This is the 'Western' side of Birkenhead shed, which, before nationalisation, was LMS and GWR joint. Seen here is WD 8F 2-10-0 No 90763 with 'Mogul' No 6374 as company.

BR 2-6-2T No 82032 hauled the 10.20am Chester-Birkenhead train. I changed at Rock Ferry onto the former Mersey Railway for the short run to Birkenhead Central. Only modern LMS-designed stock was seen, both in service and at the car sheds.

**Birkenhead shed:** Since the last visit DM 0-6-0 shunters have replaced the veteran GWR '2021' 0-6-0PT, while GWR engines are no longer stationed here and only a handful of visitors from that region were recorded. Some BR 2-6-2T and 2-6-4T are now on the allocation, in place of GWR '41XX' 2-6-2Ts.

The 66 engines seen were of a wide variety, as follows: BR 0-6-0DM No 11114/16/17/18/19/24/44/45/46/48 and D2504; BR 9F 2-10-0 No 92045 (6F); 'M of S' 2-10-0 No 90763 (12A); 'M of S' 2-8-0 No 90591; BR Class 4 2-6-4T Nos 80062/3/90; BR Class 2 2-6-2T Nos 84000/03; LMS 8F 2-8-0 Nos 48135/55 (8E), 48249 (8A), 48260, 48323 (8C), 48408, 48693

(5B) and 48752; LMS Class 5 4-6-0 No 45198; LMS Class 5 2-6-0 Nos 42929 (3D) and 42941; Stanier 2-6-0 Nos 42958/69/78; LMS Class 4 2-6-4T Nos 42447/93 and 42602/08; LMS Class 3 2-6-2T Nos 40076/78, 40101/02/16/ 21/31/44 and 40202/09; LMS Class 2 2-6-2T Nos 41226 and 41322; LMS Class 3 0-6-0T Nos 47324 47431/97, 47507/30/65 and 47627/74/77; LMS Class 2 0-6-0T Nos 47160/64; LMS 0F 0-4-0ST Nos 47005/09; LNER 'J39' 0-6-0 No 64718 (9G); LNER 'J92' 0-6-0ST No 68063 (6F); GWR '47XX' 2-8-0 No 4701; and GWR '43XX' 2-6-0 No 6374.

**Wrexham shed:** After returning to Chester behind a 2-6-4T, the 3.40pm from Chester was used as far as Wrexham, with a 'Hall' at the head. At Wrexham the first visit was to the former LNER shed now controlled by the Western Region and with a motley allocation of BR, GWR and LMS engines. There were 21 on shed, all steam, as follows: BR Class 3 2-6-2T Nos 82000/20/31; LMS Class 3 2-6-2T Nos 40085/86, 40110, and Class 2 Nos 41231/85; LMS Class 4 2-6-4T No 42372 (84G); GWR 0-6-2T Nos 5606/51, 6610; GWR 0-6-0 No

30 August 1959: These 206hp 0-6-0 diesel-mechanicals at Birkenhead had replaced the pannier tanks and 'Jinties' formerly used for local shunting. No D2504 is nearest.

3204 (in store); LNER 'J39' No 64745 (9G); and GWR 0-6-0PT Nos 1618/63/69, 3760, 4683, 8734 and 9610.

Outside were the rusty and derelict remains of two small industrial tank locos, which were there nine years ago, in 1950!

**Croes Newydd shed:** This is largely for use by freight and shunting engines, and 41 were noted. With the exception of BR No 82021 (84K) they were all of GWR origin as follows: 'Manor' 4-6-0 No 7817; '43XX' 2-6-0 Nos 5319/39/78, 6307/16/39/92, 7310/13/39; '90XX' 4-4-0 No 9014; '28XX' 2-8-0 Nos 2840/55; '22XX' 0-6-0 Nos 2244/64/66/75/94; '56XX' 0-6-2T Nos 6611/15/31/32/74/94/96; '57XX' 0-6-0PT Nos 3749, 5774, 3689, 9669; '64XX' 0-6-0PT Nos 6405, 7403/14/28/31/ 33/40/42; and '16XX' 0-6-0PT Nos 1635/60.

From Wrexham to Gobowen 'Hall' No 6932 was on the 6.14pm (a Chester-Wolverhampton

30 August 1959: In the shed yard at Wrexham Croes Newydd, locos on view are WR '43XX' 2-6-0s and '22XX' 0-6-0s.

semi-fast) and 0-4-2T No 1458 was working the auto-train from Gobowen to Oswestry.

## MONDAY 31 AUGUST 1959

The Oswestry-Whitchurch line, joined at Ellesmere by a branch from Wrexham, is the most easterly section of the Cambrian Railways. The 8.05am from Oswestry on which I travelled consisted of three corridor carriages hauled by 2-6-0 No 46518. There are seven weekday trains in this direction, one of which carries through carriages from Aberystwyth to Crewe and Shrewsbury, with an additional early morning train as far as Ellesmere. The eight Saturday trains include one at the height of the summer season from Aberystwyth to Manchester, which misses all intermediate stations. This is a reasonably good service for a line that serves a sparsely populated area.

Whitchurch, on the Shrewsbury-Crewe line, has one through platform and bay for northbound trains and an island platform for southbound traffic. There are numerous sidings and a disused LNWR four-road engine shed.

The train on which I travelled as far as Nantwich was a two-car diesel set, well patronised. The GWR branch to Wellington diverges just south of the station, and serves an agricultural area with only one town of any consequence, Market Drayton. Here,

somewhat surprisingly, the GWR and North Staffordshire Railway met, with a branch from Silverdale, near Stoke-on-Trent, which closed to passenger traffic in May 1956. There are six trains each way daily, with an extra working between Wellington and Market Drayton. There are seven stations and six halts, those trains making all 13 intermediate stops being allowed about 72 minutes for the 27½ miles from Nantwich to Wellington.

My train was the 9.30am from Crewe, due at Wellington at 10.43 am, with two non-corridors behind 2-6-2T No 4158. A fair complement of people made the journey though there was little intermediate activity save at Market Drayton.

A brief visit was made to the small shed at Wellington, which is populated entirely by BR and WR 2-6-2Ts and WR 0-6-0PTs. Nos 82006, 4110, 5167, 3732 and 9741 were recorded. No 5167 came off shed to work the 11.17am to Much Wenlock, in which I travelled. This was another two-coach train, one of two sets required to work the service of six down and seven up trains on weekdays and Saturdays. There are 11 stations and halts in this 11¼-mile journey, which is steeply graded and sharply curved for much of the distance, so the 45-50-minute time allowance is not so liberal as might be thought. The branch originally continued to join the Shrewsbury-Hereford line at Marsh Farm Junction, just

31 August 1959: A Birkenhead to Birmingham train calls at Wellington, with 4-6-0 No 4948 *Northwick Hall* in charge.

north of Craven Arms. It was closed to passenger traffic beyond Much Wenlock in January 1952, but may still be used for freight trains as far as Longville. All passenger services are to be withdrawn later this year.

The branch diverges from the Wolverhampton main line a mile or so south of Wellington and turns sharply southwards. At the first station, Ketley, and at the next halt, Lawley Bank, considerable crowds joined the train. A goods spur from Madeley Junction on the main line swings in at Lightmoor Platform, to form a triangle, and soon afterwards, after a sharp reverse curve through a steep, wooded valley at Coalbrookdale, the Severn Valley line is crossed at Buildwas. Here our crowd of passengers disembarked and I was almost the only passenger for the rest of the journey.

At Buildwas we crossed with the up train, hauled by an 0-6-0PT, and we ran past the single platform and backed into it so that the two trains stood tail-to-tail. There is only another one halt in the remaining 3¼ miles to Much Wenlock, a pretty station with single platforms and loop, with a small shed and siding beyond it

Before leaving again at 1.00pm with the same engine and train, an 0-6-0PT, No 4693, arrived on a short freight train. 'Castle' No 5045 hauled the 2.08pm ex-Wellington to Shrewsbury, this being the 11.10am Paddington-Birkenhead express.

The next stage of the journey was made on the 3.05pm Shrewsbury-Cardiff diesel express, two three-car buffet units. A fast run was made to Ludlow, with a stop at Craven Arms, and by

31 August 1959: Shrewsbury station was busier and more impressive in steam days than in its present guise. Spotters are entranced by No 7033 *Hartlebury Castle* on the 'Cambrian Coast Express'.

contrast the Ludlow-Tenbury Wells train, reversing at Woofferton, comprised a single auto 'compartment' coach propelled by 0-4-2T No 1455. During the wait at Ludlow 'Hall' No 5954 (71A) came through light. Another light engine, which ran very fast through Woofferton, was 2-8-0 No 90585 (86C).

The single line across country from Woofferton on the Shrewsbury-Hereford route to Bewdley, for Kidderminster or Hartlebury, is worked in two sections, making an end-on junction at the small two-platform station at Tenbury Wells. Like the Shrewsbury-Hereford line, the Woofferton-Tenbury section was originally LNWR/GWR joint property.

Railcar No W22 was operating the Tenbury-Bewdley service. There are four westbound and five eastbound trains on weekdays on this section, connections at Tenbury varying considerably. The country served is densely forested and thinly populated. The largest station is Cleobury Mortimer, junction for the Ditton Priors light railway; this once had its own two 0-6-0Ts, which became GWR Nos 25/26.

The day's travel ended in another WR railcar, from Bewdley to Kidderminster. Near the latter station an 0-4-0ST *BSC No 2* was at work outside a British Sugar Corporation factory.

**Kidderminster shed:** Of 14 engines noted, the following were in store: Nos 2206, 3217, 5110, 8106 and 9475/80. The others on shed were Nos 6314/88, 3207, 4153, 5179, 8101, 7700 and 8718. Naturally much of the work for the 2-6-2Ts has vanished now that many local passenger workings are dieselised.

## MONDAY 1 SEPTEMBER 1959

Until leaving Dudley en route for London, all today's travels were made in BR diesel railcars. The first was the 8.50am ex-Kidderminster on a Hereford-Worcester-Birmingham semi-fast duty, a three-car set. This was used only to Stourbridge Junction, typically GWR with two island platforms and adjacent sidings. Here a single car was waiting on the shuttle service between the Junction and Town stations, about

half a mile apart. The latter has a single platform, but the tracks run beyond, perhaps to a goods yard.

The shed contained only 24 engines (including one 0-6-0D) and two WR diesel railcars (Nos W8/15). There were two 'Halls', two '28XX' 2-8-0s, three '63XX' 2-6-0s, one '22XX' 0-6-0, five '51XX' 2-6-2Ts, three '66XX' 0-6-0Ts, five '64XX' 0-6-0PTs, and two '57XX' 0-6-0PTs. Many more of the latter were out shunting various yards in the district, and a few of these were glimpsed en route.

Returning to the Junction station, a Cardiff-Birmingham railcar set was used for the non-stop run to Snow Hill, mostly through industrial districts with frequent slowings for junctions. The main line is joined at Handsworth Junction, and there is also a spur connecting with the LMR New Street-Wolverhampton main line, at Smethwick.

Neither Snow Hill nor New Street stations proved interesting, nearly all local passenger workings into both stations being performed by diesel railcars.

The 12.55pm Birmingham-Dudley train was a single well-filled railcar. The main line is used as far as Swan Village, from which a spur curves round to Dudley Port (Low Level) on the former LNWR Walsall-Dudley line.

Dudley has two island platforms; one is used by the 'main line' (ie Wolverhampton and Stourbridge Junction line) trains, and the other by the diesel railcars on the Birmingham service and on the Dudley Port and Walsall services.

The Wolverhampton-Paddington Express, 2.30pm ex-Dudley, had 'Hall' No 5927 to Worcester, whence 'Castle' No 7030 took over. The load was five corridor coaches only, with which a fast timing of 1 hour from Oxford is scheduled. This was nearly achieved in spite of a very bad slowing at Hayes where a bridge is under repair, and a slow approach from Old Oak. The Reading-Slough section produced some very high speeds.

In the four days a mileage of 625 was covered, of which 192 were new, or nearly one-third. Forty-three engines were 'copped', of which 15 were GWR or LMS.

# INDEX

Aberdeen Ferryhill shed
41; Kittybrewster shed
40, 41
Alston 82
Amlwch branch 47, 52,
55-56
Ashford 105, 108
Ashington 81, 82

Ballachulish 43
Ballater 39-41
Ballymena 11, 12, 13
Ballymoney 12
Ballyshannon 9
Balquhidder 43
Banchory 39
Bangor (N Ireland) 16
Bangor (N Wales) 52, 55,
56
Bargoed 63
Barking 68
Barmouth 49-50
Barnard Castle 80
Barry shed 65, 66
Basingstoke 83
Bath (S&D) 8
Bathgate shed 45
Battersby 74, 76, 77
Battersea shed 2, 18-19,
57, 60
Bedford 119
Belfast & County Down
Railway 12
Belfast Adelaide shed 16,
17; Victoria Street 16;
York Road 11, 12, 14-15
Bere Alston 93
Bewdley 120, 126
Birkenhead shed 122-123
Bishop Auckland 80
Blaenau Ffestiniog branch
47

Blaydon 27-28
Blyth 81
Boston (Lincs) 109
Brecon & Merthyr line 63
Brighton shed 8
Buildwas 120-121, 125
Bundoran Junction 9

Caernarfon 50
Caerphilly 63
Cairnie Junction 39
Callander & Oban line 43
Callington branch 93-94
Calstock 94
Cardiff Bute Road 61, 63;
Canton shed 65, 67;
Clarence Road 61
Carlisle 27, 29
Chard 84
Chester 8, 56, 121;
Northgate shed 121-
122
Chester & Holyhead line
46-47
Clapham Junction 26
Cleobury Mortimer 126
Coleraine 12
Colwyn Bay 48
Comrie 43
Connel Ferry 43
Conwy 52
Corrour 34
Corwen 49
Coryton branch 63-64
County Donegal Railways
9
County School 114
Crewe 48, 56, 121
Crianlarich 34, 43
Cricklewood shed 7, 20
Croes Newydd shed 123,
124

Culmstock 89

Dalston Junction 22
Darlington 7, 75, 76, 77,
78, 80
Dawlish 92
Denbigh 49
Dereham 114
Dingwall 35, 36
Donegal 9-10
Dornoch 37, 38
Douglas (IoM) 50-51
Dowlais 63, 64
Dudley 126
Dunblane 43
Dundee shed 42
Dunfermline 30, 32, 33
Dungeness 105
Durham 80

East Grinstead 97
Eastleigh shed 8
Ebbw Junction shed 65,
67
Edinburgh, Dalry Road
shed 29, 30; Haymarket
shed 33; Seafield shed
29, 30; South Leith shed
30; St Margarets shed
30-31
Ellesmere Port 121
Enniskillen 9
Evesham 120
Exeter St David's 86-89
Exmouth Junction shed
89, 91

Fakenham 114
Ferndale 64
Ffestiniog Railway 50
Forres 39

Fort William 34

Gaerwen 56
Georgemas Junction 38
Glasgow, Eastfield shed
33; Parkhead shed 33;
Polmadie shed 8, 45
Gleneagles 43
Glenfinnan Viaduct 35
Gorton (Manchester) shed
8
Grangemouth shed 44, 45
Greenock 33
Gunnislake 94

Haltwhistle 82
Harrogate 74
Hawick 29
Helmsdale 38
Helsby 121
Hemyock branch 89, 90
Hexham 28, 81, 82
Higham Ferrers branch
117, 119
Highworth branch 26
Hitchin 98-99
Holyhead 52-53
Holywell Town branch
47, 56
Hooton 121
Horncastle branch 110
Hornsey shed 70
Hull Dairycoates shed 8
Hythe 105, 106

Inveramsay 39
Invergordon 36
Inverness 36, 39
Isle of Man railways 50-
51

Keith 39

Kettering 48
Kidderminster shed 126
Kidsgrove 48
Killin branch 43
Killybegs 10
Kingham 120
Kings Lynn 115, 116
Kinnaber Junction 42
Kittybrewster 40, 41
Knaresborough 74
Kyle of Lochalsh 35-36

Larne 16-17
Launceston branch 91, 93
Letterkenny 11
Lincoln 110
Lisburn 16
Llanberis 53
Llandaff 63
Llandudno 49ff
Lochluichart 35
Loftus 77
London Broad Street 69;
    Fenchurch Street 21;
    Liverpool Street 69;
    Victoria 23, 26
Londonderry 10, 12;
    Pennyburn shed 11
Londonderry & Lough
    Swilly Railway 11
Lydford 93

Macduff branch 39
Machen 62, 63
Maerdy branch 64
Mallaig 34, 35
Malton 71, 72, 73
March shed 8
Market Drayton 124
Melmerby 74
Menai Bridge Junction 50
Merthyr Tydfil 63
Middlesbrough 77, 78
Middleton branch 80

Monkseaton 82
Much Wenlock 124, 125

Neasden shed 7, 20
Neville Hill shed 8
New Romney 105-108
New Romney &
    Littlestone on Sea 107
Newark 111
Newbiggin 81, 82
Newcastle-upon-Tyne 27;
    NER electrics 27
Newport Ebbw Junction
    shed 65, 67
Newsham 81, 82
Newton Abbot 84-86
Newton Heath shed 8
Nine Elms shed 8, 57-59
North Wales quarries 53-
    55
North Yorkshire Moors
    line 74
Northallerton 74, 75
Northern Counties
    Committee (N Ireland)
    12
Nottingham 111-112

Oban 43-44
Old Oak Common shed 7,
    69
Oswestry 124
Oxford shed 8

Pass of Brander 43
Penmaenmawr 52
Penrhyn slate quarry 52
Penshaw 79
Perth shed 42-43
Peterborough 109
Pickering 74
Plymouth 93
Polmont shed 44, 45
Pontypridd 64

Portadown 16
Porth 64-65
Porthmadog 50
Princetown branch 91

Rannoch Moor 34
Red Wharf Bay branch 52
Redcar 77, 78
Rhyl 49, 53
Riccarton Junction 29
Rogart 36
Rolleston Junction 111
Romney, Hythe &
    Dymchurch Railway
    105
Rugby shed 8

St Boswells 29
Saltburn 77, 78
Saltley shed 8
Scarborough 72, 73
Senghenydd 62, 63
Shildon 80
Shrewsbury 121, 125
Snowdon Mountain
    Railway 53-54
South Gosforth 27
Southwell branch 111
Spalding 109
Staithes 77
Stirling 30, 33
Stockton-on-Tees 78-79
Stoke-on-Trent 48
Stonehaven 42
Stourbridge Junction 126
Strabane 10
Stranorlar 10
Stratford (London) shed
    8, 69, 70, 100, 104
Sunderland 79
Surbiton 83
Swaffham 116
Swindon shed and Works
    8, 23-25, 67

Tain 36
Tavistock 93
Teignmouth 6, 92
Temple Mills yard 69
Tenbury Wells 126
Thames Haven branch 22
The Mound 37, 38
Thetford 116
Thorverton 90
Thurso 38
Tilbury 22
Tiverton 89
Tiverton Junction 89
Tonbridge shed 95-96
Torquay 91, 94

Uffculme 89

Victoria Park (London) 22

Watford Junction 100,
    101-104
Waverley Route 29
Wellingborough shed 117,
    118, 119
Wellington (Salop) 124,
    125
Wells-next-the-Sea 113-
    114
West Hartlepool 79
Whitby 73-74, 77
Whitchurch 124
Wick 38, 39
Willesden shed 7, 69
Wood Green 68
Woodhall Junction 110
Woofferton 126
Worcester 120
Wrexham shed 123
Wymondham 114

Yelverton 91
Yeovil Junction 83, 84
York 6, 8, 71, 74